Jón R. Hjálmarsson

# HISTORY
# OF ICELAND

*From the Settlement to the Present Day*

Revised and updated edition

FORLAGIÐ

HISTORY OF ICELAND
© Jón R. Hjálmarsson 2007

Forlagið Publishing
Reykjavík 2014

Front cover: Margrét E. Laxness
Cover photo: Sigurgeir Sigurjónsson
Maps: Jean-Pierre Biard
Printing: Oddi ehf., Iceland 🌀

1st edition 1988
2nd edition 1993
3rd edition 2007
Reprinted 2009, 2012, 2014

ISBN 978-9979-53-513-3

www.forlagid.is

# Contents

To the Reader .................... 5
Country and People ............... 6

**The Discovery of Iceland**
Ultima Thule ..................... 9
A Find of Roman Coins ............. 9
Irish Hermits .................... 10
The Nordic Expansion .............. 11
First Nordic Explorers ............... 12
The Name Iceland ................. 13

**Age of Settlement**
The First Settler .................... 14
Waves of Immigrants ............... 16
Land and Life ..................... 17

**The Icelandic Commonwealth**
Unification ....................... 20
Parliament (The Althing) ............ 21

**The Saga Age**
National Growth ................... 23
The Melting Pot ................... 24
Discovery of Greenland ............. 25
Discovery of Vínland (America) ........ 26
The Old Religion .................. 28
Christian Missionaries ............... 29
Introduction of Christianity, AD1000 .... 30
The Beginning of Christian Life ........ 32
Relations with Norway .............. 34

**The Period of Peace**
First Bishop at Skálholt .............. 36
Introduction of the Tithe ............ 37
The Bishopric at Hólar .............. 39

**New Social Structure 1118–1220**
Consequences of the Tithe ........... 41
The Art of Writing ................. 41
The First Known Writer ............. 42
The Classical Historian .............. 42
The Monasteries ................... 43
Accumulation of Power .............. 44
The Militant Church ............... 46
Two Holy Men .................... 46
A Troublesome Bishop .............. 48

**Dissolution of the Commonwealth 1220–1262**
Struggle for Dominance ............. 50
Snorri Sturluson (1179–1241) ......... 50
The Battle of Örlygsstadir ........... 52
The Slaying of Snorri Sturluson ........ 52
Gissur and Thórdur ................ 53

The Flames at Flugumýri ............. 54
The Final Phase ................... 55
The Old Treaty .................... 56
Literary Greatness ................. 57

**Under Foreign Rule**
The Turning-Point ................. 58
Earldom Abolished ................. 58
New Codes of Law ................. 59
Feudalism of the Church ............. 60
A Country to Let .................. 61
The Kalmar Union ................. 62
The Great Plague (Black Death) ........ 63
The English Century ............... 63
Acts of Violence ................... 65
Subsistence and Survival ............. 66

**The Reformation of 1550**
Approaching Protestantism ........... 68
The Last Catholic Bishops ........... 69
Lutheranism in the South ............ 70
The Lost Cause of Jón Arason ......... 72

**Consequences of the Reformation**
A Cultural Shock .................. 75
Increased Royal Power .............. 75
The Commercial Monopoly ........... 76
Superstition and Witchcraft ........... 77
Turks and other Marauders .......... 79
Absolute Monarchy in 1662 .......... 79

**National Resistance**
Printing and Publishing ............. 81
Some Poets and Writers ............. 82
Precious Manuscripts ............... 84

**The Age of Enquiry**
The Registration Commission (1702–1712) 85
Messengers of Pietism (1741–1745) ...... 86
Survey of Natural Resources (1752–1757) 86
The Committee of 1770–1771 ......... 88

**The Age of Development**
An Icelandic Bailiff (1749) ........... 89
New Industrial Workshops ........... 89
The Beginning of Reykjavík ........... 91
New Buildings of Stone ............. 91

**Hard Times**
The Laki Eruptions (1783–1784) ....... 93
The Trade Monopoly Repealed (1787) ... 94
National Institutions Abolished ......... 95
Some Literary Men ................. 96

**Unrest and Troubles**
Shipping Problems and Scarce Goods .... 97
The Takeover of 1809 .............. 98
The Union of Iceland and
Norway Dissolved ............... 100
Some Cultural Trends .............. 101

**Dawn of Freedom**
New Political Currents .............. 102
Student Idealism ................... 102
The Althing Restored (1843) ......... 103

**Struggle for Independence**
Farewell to Absolute Monarchy ....... 105
The National Convention (1851) ...... 106
A Constitutional Deadlock ........... 108
The Enforced Constitutional Law (1871)109
Free Trade (1854) ................. 110
Some Economic Growth ............. 111
Schools, Poets and Culture ........... 112

**The New Era, 1874**
The Millennial Celebration .......... 114
The Constitution of 1874 ............ 114
A Nation Awakens ................. 116
Jón Sigurdsson – The Pride of Iceland ... 118
Emigration to America .............. 120
New Currents in Literature .......... 122
The Struggle for Home Rule ......... 122

**Home Rule, 1904–1918**
Hannes Hafstein – The First Icelandic
Minister ...................... 125
Development of Communications and
Industries ..................... 125
The Arrival of the Telegraph ......... 127
Schools and Academic Education ...... 128
Research and Science .............. 129
Health and Sanitary Improvements ..... 130
Temperance Movement and Prohibition .. 131
Beginning of the Labour Movement ..... 131
Women's Rights ................... 132
Growing Patriotism ................. 133
The Draft Constitution of 1908 ........ 133
Björn Jónsson, Minister 1909–1911 ..... 135
Constitutional Amendments and the Flag 136
Iceland and World War I ............ 138
The Act of Union with Denmark, 1918 .. 140

**The Icelandic Kingdom 1918–1944**
December 1, Independence Day ........ 142
Sovereignty in Reality ............... 142
Economic Growth .................. 143
New Methods in Communication ....... 145

Politics in the Inter-War Years .......... 147
The Millennial Festival of the Althing
(1930) .......................... 151
Depression and Riots ............... 152
Growing Culture and Art ............ 153
Iceland and World War II ............ 155
The British Occupation of Iceland (1940). . 155
Americans Replace the British ......... 156
The Union Treaty Revoked ........... 158

**The Republic of Iceland**
The Proclamation of the Republic, 1944 .. 160
Presidents of the Republic ............ 161
Political Parties in the Republic ......... 164
Governments under the Republic ....... 166
The Banking Collapse of 2008.......... 170

**Iceland and the World**
The United Nations ................. 171
The Keflavík Treaty, 1946 ............ 171
The Marshall Aid, 1948 .............. 172
Membership of NATO, 1949 .......... 173
Defence Treaty and Defence Force, 1951 . 175
The Nordic Council, 1952 ............ 177
Membership of EFTA, 1970 ........... 178
The Manuscripts Returned, 1971 ....... 179
Tourism – A New Industry ............ 180

**Territorial Waters and Cod Wars**
Fishery Limit from Three to Four Miles,
1952 .......................... 181
From Four to Twelve Miles, 1958 ....... 182
From Twelve to Fifty Miles, 1972 ....... 183
From Fifty to Two Hundred Miles, 1975 .. 185

**Industries and the Environment**
Agriculture ....................... 187
Fisheries ......................... 188
Energy, Industry and Service .......... 190
Communications ................... 192
Nature and Environment ............. 193

**Cultural Trends and National Life**
Schools and Education .............. 195
Church and Religion ............... 196
Literature and the Arts .............. 196
Sports and Games .................. 198
Equal Rights ...................... 199
The Festival of the Settlement, 1974 ..... 200
Lifestyles ......................... 201
New Age of Settlement .............. 202

**Bibliography** ..................... 204
**Index** .......................... 206

# To the Reader

This book, A History of Iceland, is a new work but based to a great extent upon my earlier Short History of Iceland which was published in 1988. This new history is considerably larger than its predecessor, whose entire contents have been expanded, revised and amplified, especially with regard to the events of the last two centuries.

Some years ago I used to spend my summers as a guide with foreign visitors travelling around the Icelandic countryside. As the weather was not always clear and bright enough for uninterrupted sightseeing I used some of the time to tell them tales and legends from the days of old, along with snippets of information about the history of Iceland. They often encouraged me to put into writing what I was telling them, so that they and other interested visitors could have a lasting record to take back with them and read about or refer to at leisure. And now, having done this, I sincerely hope that this book will be met with some of the interest that my fellow travellers used to show in the tales I told on numerous bus trips around Iceland, in all kinds of weather so many years ago.

I am very grateful to the many people who have been of great help to me while compiling this work. For his advice and guidance regarding the language of the text I would like to express my special thanks to Mr Bernard Scudder, who read the manuscript and made corrections or suggestions. Any errors remaining in this book are, of course, my own.

*Jón R. Hjálmarsson*

For this new and updated edition of 2007 I am grateful to many people but special thanks go to Victoria Cribb who revised the text.

*J.R.H.*

# Country and People

Iceland is an island in the North Atlantic Ocean, west of Norway, east of Greenland and to the north of the British Isles. Its exact location is between 13° 20' and 24° 32' west and 63° 24' and 66° 32' north, and therefore just skirting the Arctic Circle on its north coast. The total area of the country is 103,000 km2 or nearly 40,000 square miles. The country is situated on the Mid-Atlantic Ridge and is in fact being pulled apart by the east–west drifting of the major plates flanking the ridge. Many active volcanoes lie across the country from the southwest to the northeast and numerous eruptions gradually fill up the gap that might be caused by the spreading of these oceanic plates. In fact, the country is one of the most active volcanic regions on earth with eruptions every five years on average. Earthquakes are very common too, and geothermal springs and geysers are to be found in a great many places.

The centre of the country is mostly wasteland, volcanoes, sand and lavafields, mountains and glaciers. Most of the highland ranges from about 500 m up to 1,000 m high, but some of the mountains and glaciers reach a height of 2,000 m and the highest peak is 2,110 m, or nearly 7,000 ft. above sea level. Only about a quarter of the country is habitable, in lowlands and valleys near the coast. The rest is barren mountains and highland with very little vegetation.

The climate is cool temperate oceanic, but windy, wet and changeable. It is influenced by both the warm Gulf Stream from the south and cold Arctic currents from the north. The average January temperature is about -1°C and in July about +11°C, making the climate milder than could be expected from the country's northern location, but very unstable.

Iceland has been inhabited since the ninth century. The old Icelandic Commonwealth was established in 930, when the Althing, often described as one of the oldest surviving parliaments in the world, first met at Thingvellir. This "Saga Republic" lasted until 1262

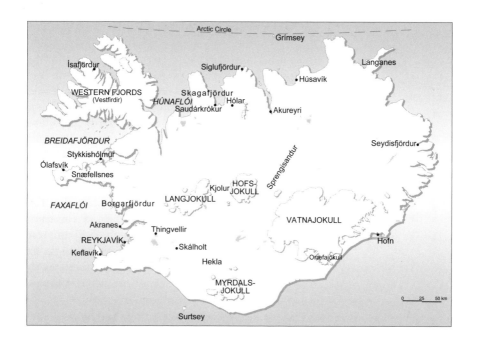

when the country submitted to the king of Norway, followed in 1380 by more than five centuries of Danish domination. The Icelanders suffered hard times but overcame poverty, famine, natural disasters, plagues, ice and fire to sever the last ties with Denmark in 1944 and establish their republic anew.

The population of Iceland is now over 300,000 and has grown very fast in recent times. The form of government is a constitutional democratic republic. Iceland's capital is Reykjavík, with more than 110,000 inhabitants. Most Icelanders belong to the Evangelical Lutheran State Church. Culturally they are both active and aware, and illiteracy is unknown. Farming was the main occupation of most people in former times, but now people have moved from the countryside into towns and villages to a great extent, and fishing and fish industries have become the mainstay of the economy. Fish products of various kinds make up the majority of exports. Aluminium, woollen goods and sundry other items make up the rest.

Iceland is a somewhat barren country and has neit-

7

her rich agricultural land nor minerals, but nevertheless has a number of plentiful resources, such as bounteous fishing grounds, and energy in the form of the
hydroelectric potential of its numerous rivers and
waterfalls, along with a lot of geothermal heat. But of
all its resources the most vital for this young nation is
enough well-educated and industrious people to take
care of everything that today's modern welfare state
demands.

   This history of Iceland is an attempt to tell the story
of the Icelanders through the centuries and the
struggle of the people against the elements and foreign rulers. The Icelanders have always been a peaceful nation and have never been involved in any real
warfare with other nations. But their history is the history of unceasing battles. They have suffered many
losses, but they have survived and, in the final analys-
is, they have won.

*Reykjavík today.*

# The Discovery of Iceland

## Ultima Thule

Iceland is not only geologically a very young country, but also the last in Europe to be settled. It was first settled in the Middle Ages when all neighbouring countries had been inhabited for thousands of years. The history of Iceland is therefore different from most other countries in that it has no prehistoric period.

But the country may have been discovered in much earlier times and we have some tales and legends that point in that direction. In Greek and Roman sources we read about Thule or Ultima Thule, the northernmost island of the world, six days by sea north of the British Isles and very near to the frozen ocean. This piece of information is derived from the explorer Pytheas of Massalia, or Marseilles, who lived about 300BC. It has not been proved that this northern island was Iceland, but Thule is the oldest name of the country and was used for some time in the Middle Ages.

## A Find of Roman Coins

In recent times several Roman copper coins have been found in excavations in the southeast and south of Iceland, dating from a little before AD300. It is hard to guess how these old coins could have reached Iceland. Nordic settlers may have brought them with them when they came over in the ninth or tenth century, but they may also have found them when looking for traces of former habitation in the country. We can therefore imagine that seafaring people from the Roman Empire, and in that case most probably from Britain, which was a Roman colony at the time this money was in use, might have come to the country about AD300 or a little later. But whatever happened, these coins will remain something of a mystery until more is learned about their provenance.

*Roman coins from about AD300.*

## Irish Hermits

The Irish, who were Christianized early, began in the Middle Ages to seek out remote places and faraway islands where they could serve God in solitude. Men of God began sailing the North Atlantic in their tiny skin boats which were called currachs. In these voyages they discovered the Faroe Islands around the middle of the seventh century and settled down there with their sheep. And these seafaring recluses sailed farther and probably reached Iceland, or Thule as they called it, about the middle or at least in the latter half of the eighth century. This date may have been even earlier, since the great English scholar, the Venerable Bede (674–735), mentions Thule in his writings.

Dicuilus, a learned Irish monk who taught at a school in France, wrote that he had been told by some Irish priests that they had lived for a while in a remote country which they called Thule and said was uninhabited. They had been there around 795 and stayed for about six months. They also told him that in midsummer there was bright daylight during both day and night, and it was so light that they could even pick lice from their shirts at midnight.

It is obvious from these records that the Irish were in Iceland nearly a century before the Norse settlement began, if not earlier, although it is not certain whether they ever established a lasting settlement. Most probably they arrived sporadically and stayed for varying lengths of time. But it is clear that they were in Iceland when the first Nordic Vikings arrived. In the Book of Icelanders which Ari Thorgilsson the Learned wrote about the earliest history of Iceland, he mentions the Irish who were there at that time, and were called "papar" or fathers by the Vikings. After the Norse settlement began, the Irish monks either went away because they would not live with the heathens, or were driven away from their lands by the new settlers. Probably they left in a hurry, for they are said to have left behind Irish books, bells and croziers. Another historical work, the Book of Settlements, mentions the Irish too and some places are named

*Irish cross dating from the early 10th century.*

10

*The settlers of Iceland braved the ocean on ships like this.* after them. But as their settlement was impermanent and abandoned, these Irish hermits did not have any lasting influence on the history of Iceland. It seems most likely that the Norsemen first learned from the Irish about the faraway land of Thule in the northwest.

## The Nordic Expansion

The Viking Age in the Nordic countries – Denmark, Norway and Sweden – started in the eighth century and lasted until the eleventh. In this period these Nordic nations were practically at war with the rest of the world. They were better shipbuilders, more daring seamen and tougher warriors than their neighbours, in addition to the fact that the population of these countries had grown so much that there was hardly room and opportunities for them all at home.

These Norsemen then became Vikings or pirates, attacking and raiding other countries. The first recorded Viking raid on England was in 793, and on Ireland in 795. These Vikings were cruel and terrible enemies and a great threat to Christians, for the Norsemen were still heathen at this time. After a while the Vikings began to settle abroad. The Swedes crossed the Baltic Sea and established a Viking state in what is now Russia and the Ukraine, while the Danes and Norwegians established a number of such states in Ireland, England, Scotland, France and elsewhere. The Norwegians settled at an early date on the islands north of Scotland. In the first half of the ninth century they reached the Faroe Islands and settled down there. Meaning literally "Sheep Islands", this name is probably derived from the great number of sheep which the Irish had brought there.

## First Nordic Explorers

About the middle of the ninth century or shortly after, a Norwegian named Naddoddur was sailing from Norway to the Faroe Islands. As often happened on the ocean, he and his men lost their way and could not find the place they had set off for. Instead, they headed much farther towards the northwest and suddenly found a land they had not known about before. They had come to the east coast of Iceland. Wanting to know more about this country, they explored the surroundings for a while. Eventually they climbed a high mountain to look farther for smoke or other signs of human habitation, but failing to see anything of that kind, they soon turned back. But before they left, some snow fell on the mountains. Naddoddur then gave this new country the name "Snowland".

The next Viking who sailed to Iceland was Gardar Svavarsson, a man of Swedish origin. To discover more about the country he sailed around it and found out that it was an island. Since this "round trip" took some time, he and his men stopped at a bay on the north coast where they stayed through the winter. They built some houses there and this place has borne the name Húsavík or House Bay ever since. While they were wintering there, a man named Náttfari and a slave and a slave girl broke away from Gardar and his men, built themselves a house and settled down in a valley near Húsavík. But either because his settlement was somewhat casual or because he was not noble enough, Náttfari has never been counted as the first settler in Iceland. Gardar finished his circumnavigation and sailed away. He named this big island "Gardarshólmi", or Gardar's Island, after himself, and the name continued to be used for a while afterwards.

## The Name Iceland

A Norwegian Viking, Flóki Vilgerdarson, later nicknamed Raven-Flóki, was the third visitor from the Nordic countries. He set out deliberately to seek this new land of Gardarshólmi, taking with him his family, friends and household with the intention of settling down there. Flóki was a devout believer in the old pagan religion and worshipped ravens, taking three with him on his ship. Legend says that when he thought he was somewhere near land he released the ravens one by one so that they could show him the way there. The first of them flew back, the second flew up into the air and down to the ship again, but the third flew forward and led him to the land.

Flóki and his men sailed close to the south coast, rounded the Reykjanes peninsula and headed northward until they found a fjord in the northwest part of the country where the land was fertile and nature bounteous. All summer the men were busy fishing, hunting and gathering eggs, and forgot to make any hay for the winter. With no fodder during the cold and severe winter that followed, animals died. When spring came and the weather began to improve, Flóki climbed to the top of a mountain, looked down on the other side and saw a fjord full of ice. Bitter and frustrated, he gave the country the name of Iceland, which it has borne ever since.

After another year in the west of Iceland Flóki sailed back to Norway. He talked badly of this new land in the west, but some of the party who had been with him were of a different opinion and described it as dripping with milk and honey. And maybe Flóki changed his opinion too, since many years later he came back to Iceland where he remained for the rest of his life.

# Age of Settlement

## The First Settler

News soon spread to nearby countries of the new un-inhabited island Flóki and the others had found to the west with plenty of land for anyone who would go there. Word reached two young men in the southwest of Norway: Ingólfur Arnarson and Hjörleifur Hród-marsson, close friends and foster-brothers. Returning to Norway as rich men after Viking adventures abroad, they got into a quarrel with the sons of a pow-erful earl in the neighbourhood, and killed two of them in battle. The earl, of course, was furious, and forced them to give him all their land as compensa-tion. And with no land to live on in Norway any long-er, they had to find it elsewhere.

The foster-brothers made an expedition to Iceland to see what it looked like, stayed for a while in the southeast part of the country and explored the surro-undings. Finding out that this was a good and fertile land, they made up their minds to emigrate there from Norway. Back home again, they sold everything they could not take with them and loaded their ships with their families, freemen, slaves, animals, food and implements of all kinds, and sailed to Iceland about the year AD870.

Hjörleifur seems to have been a liberal man in reli-gious matters, but Ingólfur was a devoted adherent of the old faith. Wanting the gods to tell him where he should live in the new country, when he was not far off the coast of Iceland he threw overboard the high-seat pillars he had taken with him from the old house in Norway and said he would settle down where the gods willed them to drift ashore. Soon afterwards they reached land. Ingólfur settled first at Ingólfshöfdi in the southeast, not far from what is now the national park of Skaftafell. But Hjörleifur sailed farther west and settled at Hjörleifshöfdi on the middle of the south coast, near the spot where the little town of Vík is now.

*Ingólfur Arnarsson, first settler of Iceland, statue by Einar Jónsson.*

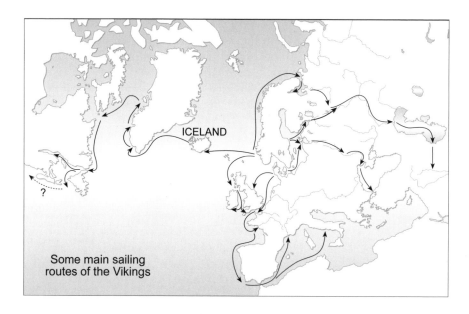

Some main sailing
routes of the Vikings

The following spring Hjörleifur ordered a number
of Irish slaves, whom he had captured on a Viking trip
and taken with him, to plough a field and sow some
grain. But instead they revolted, killing Hjörleifur and
all his freemen, and sailed, taking the women with
them, to some islands off the south coast, where they
settled. Some time later Ingólfur came on a visit and
found his foster-brother and his men all dead. Pitying
them deeply, he said such things happened to men
who were not devoted enough to the old religion.
Then he sailed to the islands, killed all the slaves and
rescued the women. One of them was his sister Helga,
who had been Hjörleifur's wife. Since the Vikings sometimes referred to the Irish as "Westmen", after the
position of their country on Viking sailing routes, Ingólfur called these islands Vestmannaeyjar or Westman
Islands after the fugitive slaves, and they have kept
this name ever since.

Afterwards Ingólfur moved with his people and belongings to Hjörleifshöfdi and lived there for a year.
But all the time he moved westwards along the coast
he kept on the lookout for his high-seat pillars to learn
where the gods deemed he should build his home. In
his third year in the new land he built a house under

Mt. Ingólfsfell, near what is now the town of Selfoss. The following summer the slaves he had sent to scout the shores found the pillars at last, washed up in a little bay or fjord on the southwest coast, and Ingólfur was so pleased that he gave them their freedom and some land to live on. He interpreted the find as meaning that the gods had shown him their will and brought him to this place to build his permanent home. On that spot were a great number of hot springs, which the Norsemen were not familiar with from their own country. Ingólfur named his new home Reykjavík, or "Smoky Bay", after the white steam or smoke he saw rising from the hot springs. This is now the site of the capital city of Iceland, Reykjavík.

The land Ingólfur took as his possession comprised the whole southwest part of the country, stretching from Hvalfjördur (Whale Fjord) in the west to the river Ölfusá in the east. Since this was a much bigger territory than he needed or could ever use for himself, he sold or gave away a great deal of it to friends and relatives who arrived later. It has become customary to say that Ingólfur began the settlement of Iceland in AD874, although the actual date may have been a little earlier.

## Waves of Immigrants

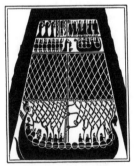

After Ingólfur Arnarson and his wife Hallveig Fródadóttir had settled down in Reykjavík, more people began to move to Iceland. The period from 870 or thereabouts to 930 is called the Age of Settlement, because in that time most inhabitable parts of the country were claimed and settled. The events of this period are recorded in old literature and other sources, of which the most comprehensive are the Book of Icelanders and the Book of Settlements. No other European nation has such clear records about its origin and background.

These earliest sources record the names of more than 400 settlers, along with their family backgrounds and details of where they came from and the places

*Vikings.* they settled down. Naturally a far greater number of

*A warrior.*

people actually moved to Iceland, for only the noblest and most prominent leaders were counted. Besides Ingólfur Arnarson in Reykjavík, some of the best known were Skallagrímur Kveldúlfsson and Audur the Deepminded in the west, Ingimundur the Old and Helgi the Lean in the north, Hrollaugur Rögnvaldsson in the east and Ketilbjörn the Old in the south. The great majority of the immigrants came from the west and southwest of Norway and some might have been from other Nordic countries, while a considerable number originated from the British Isles, especially from Ireland, Scotland and the islands to the west and north of Scotland. Intermingling in many ways, these immigrants soon built up a new nation, the Icelanders, who quickly developed distinctive customs, culture, language and literature.

There were many reasons for the wave of immigration to Iceland. In many countries there was a constant need for more land, and in some places people wanted a haven to escape from oppression and cruelty. Iceland offered them both land and freedom in abundance. In Norway at that time, King Haraldur Fairhair was uniting the country into a single state, and in the conflicts and warfare that ensued, many rich and noble men became his enemies and fled. Many others resented his constant decrees, taxation and oppression, and preferred to leave for Iceland. The king did not like this intense emigration from his country, and when his attempts to stop it failed, an agreement was made to the effect that everybody who left for Iceland should pay a tax to the king. That tax became permanent, even after the settlement period. Another factor that must be taken into account was the sudden increase in the pace of life in the Viking Age, when cruising the high seas was a quite normal activity and travelling from one country to another had become almost a part of daily life.

## Land and Life

The settlers in Iceland soon established certain rules about taking land. A man was allowed to claim land

17

*The Saga Age farm in Thjórsárdalur valley south Iceland, a reconstruction based on the Stöng ruin.*

inside a boundary defined by how many fires he could light within sight of each other in a single day. There was a different arrangement for women, who were supposed to lead a heifer for one day from sunrise to sunset around the land where they intended to stake a claim. The population of Iceland by the end of the settlement period in 930 is unknown, but it has been estimated to have been about 60,000.

The country that the settlers found looked somewhat different from the Iceland of today. The mountains and highlands, volcanoes and glaciers were very much the same, but a much greater part of the country was covered with some vegetation. In the lowlands, fjords and valleys there were vigorous birch forests, even stretching high up into the hills and mountain slopes. It has been estimated that at the beginning of the settlement two thirds of the surface of the country was covered with some vegetation and that birch forests made up the greater part of it. Now, vegetation covers only one quarter of the country and forests grow on a mere one per cent. As Iceland is an island in the ocean and very far away from all other countries, animal life was very limited. The fox was the only mammal on land, probably coming over with drift ice from Greenland, but there were great herds of seals on the beaches and many kinds of whales swam about off the coast. Birdlife was rich, especially with a great variety and number of seabirds. The rivers and lakes were full of trout and salmon and there were plenty of fish in the fjords and close to the shore. Most of the beaches, too, were covered with heaps of driftwood which could be used as building material by the newcomers.

It must have been fairly easy for the settlers to make their living in the beginning, with such an abundance of food all around. But a lot of work still had to be done before they could establish themselves permanently. First they had to build houses, and as they were farmers their next step would have been to clear forests, plough the soil and grow grass, grain and vegetables. On board their ships they had brought domestic animals such as sheep and cows, horses and pigs, poultry and geese, dogs and cats. As there was space enough, the settlers built their farms very scattered in the countryside to have large grazing grounds, which has been characteristic of rural Iceland ever since. Immigration to Iceland ebbed out for the most part about AD930, by which time a new and distinct nation had come into existence on this island in the North Atlantic.

*Archaeological excavation have revealed this design of the farmstead at Stöng, wich was laid waste by a volcanic eruption in 1104.*

1. Entrance
2. Hall
3. Living room
4. Dairy
5. Lavatory

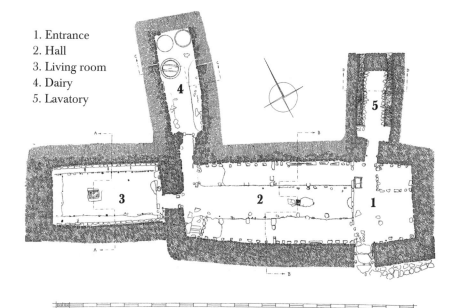

# The Icelandic Commonwealth

## Unification

The settlers in Iceland, who came in groups – comprising men, women, children, freemen and slaves – very often belonged to one big family in each part of the country. In most of these groups one particular man was the leader or chieftain, and since he was usually rich and of noble birth it was natural for him to govern his people in both secular and religious matters. Leaders of this kind laid down certain basic rules in their settlements which had to be respected, and also took care of necessary offerings to the gods at certain times of the year. For such services the people had to pay taxes which in the course of time strengthened the leaders' position, making them richer and more powerful still.

In this way a number of more or less independent principalities gradually developed, scattered around the country. In a Viking settlement this was a quite natural arrangement, for the immigrants only brought with them the customs they were used to from Norway or wherever else they had arrived from. Members of each community gathered at certain times of the year for local meetings or assemblies where they agreed upon the laws and rules that they would be governed by, and also to pass sentences upon people who violated them.

Inevitably, a considerable amount of lawlessness and warfare prevailed among families in the new Viking settlement which grew up in Iceland over a relatively short period of time. The majority of the people, however, preferred to live in peace and very soon the wisest among the leaders realized the benefit of having the same law everywhere and some kind of unified society in the country as a whole. Such ideas seem to have originated in the settlement established by Ingólfur Arnarson in Reykjavík. His son, Thorsteinn Ingólfsson, and other descendants brought about the unification of several small communities in

*Thingvellir, the Parliament Plains, where the independent Icelandic commonwealth was established in AD930.* their region, under one local assembly or parliament. A similar development seems to have taken place in some other parts of the country. In the course of time this movement spread and eventually led to the unification of all the scattered chieftainships into a single republic, and the formation of one general assembly for the whole nation. The outcome was the establishment of the independent Icelandic Commonwealth in AD930.

## Parliament (The Althing)

Once the dominant chieftains in Iceland had agreed to the idea of uniting their country into a single society, their most pressing need was to set up a legal framework for this new commonwealth. They sent a wise man, Úlfljótur, to western Norway to learn about the law and form of government in certain districts there, and after three years he returned with an ample collection of laws which he had adapted to local conditions in Iceland. Another man, Grímur Geitskör, was then sent all over Iceland to find a convenient site for the new parliament, and probably also to enlist further support for the idea of unification from as many of the leading chieftains as possible.

*Head of a bishop's crozier, from the 11th century.*

About this time a farmer living at Bláskógar (Blue Forests) on the outskirts of the Reykjavík settlement was found guilty of murdering a slave or freeman. He was sentenced to pay a fine and also to forfeit his land, which became public property. This spot was on the plains to the north of the great lake of Thingvallavatn, and it was agreed that this should become the site for the new parliament, which gathered there for the first time in AD930. There were thirty-six principalities in the country at this time, each with one chieftain who then became a member of the new assembly with the right to vote. Somewhat later, in 965, the country was divided into four quarters and the number of representatives increased to thirty-nine. With further modifications it was subsequently determined that they should be forty-eight in number. The lawspeaker was a member too, as were the two bishops of the country after the introduction of Christianity, bringing the membership to fifty-one. Each of the regular chieftains had two advisors or assistants, making the number of parliamentary representatives 147 in all.

Parliament had both legislative and judiciary power, but there was no common executive power, and this was only enforced privately. These free and independent chieftains did not want to have a king or earl above them. The fact that the country was so far away that there was little or no need for any common defence may, however, have been the main reason for the decision not to have a common leader or sovereign.

In parliament, the lawspeaker was the most powerful man. He knew the laws of the land by heart and was obliged to recite them in their entirety from the Law Rock over the course of three annual parliaments, for they were not put into writing until 1117. Parliament also had judiciary power and formed courts for each quarter of the country. In 1004 a supreme or high court was also established. But in spite of unification and the single national parliament, local government in the scattered districts remained intact and every community enjoyed a good deal of autonomy.

# The Saga Age

## National Growth

In the history of Iceland it is customary to talk about the period from the establishment of the Common-wealth in 930 until about 1030 as the Saga Age. This was a time of national and cultural growth when most of the heroic events took place which would lay the foundation for the remarkable Sagas and poetry. The Sagas lived on in oral tradition, transmitted from generation to generation, until they were committed to writing mostly in the twelfth and thirteenth centuries. But not only the Sagas blossomed in early Iceland. A great number of poets became famous too. The first and perhaps greatest of them all was the mighty warrior Egill Skallagrímsson in the tenth century. Once when in England, under sentence of death, he ransomed back his life by delivering a poem in praise of the king who was holding him. He and many other poets travelled to recite their poems at the courts of

*Warrior and poet Egill Skallagrímsson has always been one of the most popular characters in the Sagas.*

kings and earls overseas and were handsomely rewarded.

The Saga Age was an era of prosperity for the Icelanders. They had begun using the land, built up their farms and made themselves at home. For the most part they lived by farming and fishing. Many of them had their own ships and earned their living as merchants, while some also went abroad to take part in the lucrative Viking raids which were still going on in the Nordic countries. On the whole, this new nation in the North Atlantic was culturally aware, led a good, healthy life and was happy with its lot.

## The Melting Pot

Iceland's Parliament or Althing was held every year at midsummer on the spot called Thingvellir or Parliament Plains, on the north side of Lake Thingvallavatn, a showcase of natural beauty with fine vegetation and majestic volcanic rifts. The largest of these is Almannagjá or the People's Rift, where most of the parliamentary proceedings took place. These medieval men seem to have had a keen eye for nature, for they took a little river west of Parliament Plains and diverted it into the great rift to make a fine waterfall, thereby providing themselves with good fresh water on the spot and enhancing the beauty of the landscape at the same time. Many of the chieftains built camps to live in while parliament was in session, and ruins of their turfed booths can still be seen today, although others used tents. But there was no parliament building as such and most of the meetings and proceedings took place in the open air.

Not only the rich and powerful attended the parliament session. A great number of other people gathered there every year, creating in effect a sense of a national festival. There were buyers and sellers of all kinds of goods, athletes, warriors, poets, storytellers, jugglers and all manner of travellers, while many others turned up only to look and listen. Men and women from different parts of the country met, discussed common interests, invited one another to celebrations, planned marriages between their sons and daughters, and the like. It was an occasion for discussing common interests, hearing about great events at home and abroad, and for learning. All kinds of people gathered around the parliament, a full cross-section of society, making the event a true melting pot for culture, national feeling and unity.

## Discovery of Greenland

In the Saga Age the Icelanders were still a seafaring nation. Cruising the ocean was a Viking tradition and the Icelanders continued exploring the high seas and discovering new lands. Since Greenland is not very far away, it was only a matter of time before sailors who drifted west of Iceland would come into sight of this gigantic land. The first seaman known to have travelled to Greenland was Gunnbjörn Úlfsson, who reached the east coast in the tenth century. Shortly afterwards a man named Snaebjörn Galti arrived and took winter quarters there. News of the discovery spread and people grew interested in this new land.

Eiríkur Thorvaldsson, or Eric the Red as he was often called, lived in the west of Iceland. A strong warrior and daring seaman, Eric quarrelled with his neighbours and killed some of them in a battle, for which he was sentenced to three years' exile. As he had heard about this new land in the west, he put to sea to look for it some time just after 980. Soon he found it, rounded its southernmost point and explored it. He gave it the name Greenland, expecting more people to be interested in moving to join him if it had an attractive name. He eventually sailed back to Iceland, but the following summer he moved to Greenland for good with his people and household and settled down there around 986.

As Eric the Red had wished, plenty of people in Iceland were interested and emigrated to Greenland, settling down in two different regions on the west coast. The Greenland settlements flourished for a long time and the people there lived very much like the people in Iceland, although they were probably more dependent on fishing and hunting. The Greenlanders had their own legislative assembly at Gardar, which was also the seat of the bishop after Christianity had been introduced about the same time as it was in Iceland.

But over a very long period contact by sea with Greenland declined, and after the fifteenth century no ships came there for about two hundred years. Nobody really knows what happened, but after 1500 all Nordic people seem to have disappeared from their settlements. Later only Inuits were to be found in these parts. Silent ruins bear witness to this old Nordic settlement, but nothing else.

## Discovery of Vínland (America)

Leifur, the son of Eric the Red, or Leif Ericson the Lucky, was born in Iceland but moved with his father to Greenland and settled there. Like his father, Leif was an explorer and adventurer by nature. Around the time that Leif left for Greenland, another Icelandic seaman, Bjarni Herjólfsson, set off there, but lost his way and went much farther southwest than intended. He and his men sighted unfamiliar land, although Bjarni was not curious enough to stop and go ashore. Instead he turned back and eventually reached Greenland. On hearing about this new land on the other side of the ocean, Leif became interested, took over Bjarni's ship and sailed westwards to look for it some time around the year 1000. When he found it he went ashore with his men to explore, giving names to the different territories they visited. First they came to Helluland (Baffin Island), then Markland (Labrador), and after sailing south for a long time they stopped at a place they called Vínland, or Wineland, on account of what they thought were some grapes or vines growing on the ground. It is not certain if this Wineland was what is now Nova Scotia; some historians think the territories Leif visited were a good deal farther south on the east coast of North America. On his way back to Greenland Leif found some shipwrecked men

*Leifur Eiríksson, "Leif the Lucky" statue given to Iceland by the United States.*

*Ruins of the church at Hvalsey, Whales Island, in Greenland.*

on a skerry and rescued them, earning himself the nickname Leif the Lucky.

Greenlanders and Icelanders sailed to these vast and rich lands in the west for some time and news about this discovery spread. But strange to say, it did not arouse much notice or curiosity in the countries of the Vikings. It seems as if the wave of Nordic expansion had spent its force and broke at last on the east coast of North America. A few attempts were made, however, to make use of this new land and settle there. The most determined attempt was made by Icelander Thorfinnur Thórdarson and his wife Gudrídur Thorbjarnardóttir, who lived there for several years in the first decade of the eleventh century. While they were in the new settlement their son Snorri Thorfinnsson was born, who is most likely the first European born in America.

Eventually these settlers gave up trying to live in the new world and returned to Iceland. It soon became clear that they were too few against the natives, who were Indians or Inuits or both, and after a series of battles the Icelanders gave up and left. It would be nearly five centuries before America was again visited by a European, this time by Columbus, and colonized. But we could play with the notion that had the Icelanders not been too few or the natives too many at this time, we would probably have been able to travel across the North-American continent today and only need to speak Icelandic with the people we met on our way from the Atlantic to the Pacific Ocean. We should also keep in mind that Columbus, as he says himself, visited Iceland on board an English ship in 1477. In all likelihood he heard from learned Icelanders of Greenland in the west and the vast Vínland farther southwest. Who knows if he did not get the idea of looking for Asia on the other side of the Atlantic from this Iceland voyage?

## *The Old Religion*

At the beginning, the Icelanders were heathen for the most part. In the Age of Settlement there were nonetheless a good number of Christian settlers, for those who came from Ireland, England and Scotland, or had lived in other Viking settlements, had been influenced by the Christian faith and some of them had been baptized. The heathen majority believed in the old Nordic deities like the almighty Ódinn (Woden), the strong thunder-god Thor and a number of other gods and goddesses, as all the Teutonic peoples had done in former times.

Old sources tell us that the gods were worshipped in special temples or in the halls of the biggest farms. Human sacrifices are not mentioned in the sources, and animals, mostly horses, seem to have been the victims at these religious feasts, when the sacrificial blood was smeared on the walls, and the meat was cooked and eaten. Such religious feasts were held at certain times of the year and conducted by the local chieftains or priests, who in turn were given a very powerful position in their community.

After the unification of the nation and the establishment of the single national assembly of the Althing in 930, the old faith seems to have grown stronger. At the same time Christian influences waned and disappeared for the most part. The structure of power in the new commonwealth favoured the heathen religion, with the most powerful leaders of society basing their position and authority on a religious foundation. The medieval republic of Iceland was therefore an almost completely heathen society almost to the end of the tenth century.

## Christian Missionaries

As the Christian religion was advancing in other Nordic countries in the tenth century and other countries in Northern Europe had already been Christianized, it was quite natural that missionaries should visit Iceland as well. A Saxon missionary bishop, Friedrich, and his Icelandic assistant, Thorvaldur the Far-Travelled, were the first to arrive. They worked from 981 to 986 with some success, especially in the northern quarter, but because Thorvaldur killed men in a battle during their travels they were forced to leave the country.

*Figurine of Thór, the mighty thunder-god, found in North Iceland.*

A few years after these missionaries left, the Viking chief Ólafur Tryggvason became king of Norway. He had been baptized and was very zealous in his Christian mission. After coming to power and more or less completing the Christianization of his own people in Norway, he directed his efforts towards spreading the faith in Norse settlements abroad such as the Orkneys, Shetland, Faroe Islands, Iceland and Greenland. He dispatched missionaries far and wide, leaving no stone unturned for the Christian cause, and was successful in his efforts too, although his time was cut short when he was killed in battle against the Swedes, Danes and his own countrymen of Norway, in the autumn of AD1000.

King Ólafur's first missionary to Iceland was Stefnir Thorgilsson, a native of Iceland, who started by attacking and breaking down heathen temples, and was promptly exiled. Next, the King sent a Flemish priest named Thangbrandur, who had reached Norway via England. He managed to baptize several of the noble Icelandic chieftains, but as he could not tolerate any opposition and killed several men who spoke against him, he too had to leave the country. Back in Norway, he told the King that the Icelanders were bad by nature and that it was doubtful if they ever could be Christianized at all.

At these words the King flew into a rage and threatened to mutilate and kill every heathen Icelander who could be found in Norway at that time. Before he could make good his threats, two Christian chieftains, Gissur the White and Hjalti Skeggjason, came to visit him from Iceland. They tried hard to calm him down and negotiate about religious matters, and ended up by promising that the Icelanders would be Christianized in the very near future, whereupon the delighted king abandoned his plans for a massacre, although he kept a few hostages all the same. Through their agreement with the King, Gissur and Hjalti were actually working for the benefit of their country and serving its interests, because good relations with Norway were of vital importance for Iceland from historical and above all from commercial points of view, and for many other reasons besides. It was also hard for them to guess exactly what the king would have done if no agreement had been made. Another factor to be taken into account was that these two Icelandic chieftains had themselves been baptized and naturally wanted to strengthen the Christian cause in their own country.

*Wooden statue of Christ from the latter half of the 12th century.*

## Introduction of Christianity, AD1000

The two chiefs who had negotiated with the King of Norway came back to Iceland in due time for the parliament of the year 1000. People had gathered at the assembly in great numbers, but were divided into many disputing factions. The most extreme heathens stood firmly against all changes in religious matters, while the Christian group was equally eager in its mission. But a great many people seem to have been tolerant and realistic in their religious views, and desired above all to preserve peace and unity in the country. When religious war seemed on the verge of breaking out between the two factions, the wisest of the chieftains took an initiative towards a compromise. They agreed to choose Thorgeir of Ljósavatn (Bright Lake) in the north of the country, a heathen who had taken

*Death of King Ólafur Haraldsson of Norway in the battle of Stiklastad in 1030, illumination from the Flatey manuscript.*

a moderate stand on the issue, to act as lawspeaker and arbitrator, and they promised to obey his verdict.

Thorgeir felt the heavy burden of his lot. He went to his booth and lay down under a hide for the whole of that day and the next night to meditate on this knotty question. In the meantime the pagans met and discussed seriously if they should not sacrifice two men from each quarter of the country, in order to make sure of the gods' support for their cause. The Christians mocked them, saying that in their circle two men had already volunteered to give their lives for Christ and his victory.

Next morning the lawspeaker rose from his bed and ordered all present to gather at the Law Rock. He then delivered from it what is probably the most important speech ever made in the country's history. He said it was intolerable for the people to be divided and no longer have one law in the land to live by. With a series of arguments he tried to calm down the extremists on both sides, saying it was not wise to leave the making of decisions in the hands of those who wanted the most of everything. Let us rather come to a compromise, he said, whereby both sides are given something but remain united with one law, as one undivided nation in one country, for if we divide the law, we will break the peace.

After this Thorgeir delivered his verdict, that all people should be Christian and be baptized. However, worship of the old gods was still allowed in private, as was the eating of horse meat and the exposure of children at birth. Probably neither the Christians nor the pagans were pleased with his verdict, but since it had now become the law of the land it had to be obeyed. A great many people were baptized on the spot in the cold water at the parliament site, and others on their way back home where rather more comfortable warm geothermal water could be found.

Thorgeir was a heathen himself when, in his capacity as lawspeaker, he determined that everybody should be Christian, and had of course to be baptized at once. Legend says that when this wise and moderate man returned home from this historic parliament, he took all his statues of the old heathen gods from their temple, carried them to a nearby river and threw them into a mighty waterfall. Since then this fall has always been named Godafoss, or the Gods' Waterfall, and is one of the most beautiful in the country.

*Goðafoss,*
*The Gods' Waterfall.*

## The Beginning of Christian Life

The introduction of Christianity in Iceland was a peaceful and almost unique historical event. It was quite different from the prolonged conflicts, warfare and bloodshed which customarily accompanied Christianization in most other countries. This peaceful settlement arose probably more for political than religious reasons. But the Icelanders were ill-prepared for life and work in the Roman Catholic Church at that time. There were very few churches then, hardly any clergy and no separate code of ecclesiastical law to live by.

Soon the chieftains, who earlier had been leaders in heathen religious ceremonies, began to build churches and hire priests to handle baptism of children and

*Episcopal consecration in medieval times.*

burial of the dead in consecrated ground. It helped a good deal at this time that a number of foreign priests, mostly English and German, came to the country to serve God and work. A few missionary bishops came over too, and some of them stayed for many years, making a significant contribution towards establishing the new religion. Some of the bishops were English, and there were considerable English influences on church life and even the language, some of which are still noticeable.

But on the whole the Church was weak in these first decades of Christianity and the situation did not essentially improve until the first Icelandic bishop came to office in 1056. The exceptions from Christian practice regarding private worship of the old gods, eating horse meat and exposure of infants were abolished as early as 1016, largely due to the persuasive efforts of the Norwegian King Ólafur Haraldsson, who afterwards sent the Icelanders a bell and timber for a new church that was erected on the parliament site at Thingvellir about 1020. Christian influences became stronger and helped foster less aggressive and more civilized social attitudes. For instance, the old custom of fighting duels at Thingvellir during parliament was prohibited early in the eleventh century. Christian influences were also one reason why slavery declined and disappeared in the eleventh and early twelfth centuries.

## Relations with Norway

Despite Iceland's location in the middle of the Atlantic and distance from other countries, foreign kings tried from an early date to gain some influence and even acquire the country. In the Age of Settlement itself, Haraldur Fairhair, King of Norway, sent his envoy Uni Gardarsson on a mission to Iceland to persuade the people to submit to his rule. The King had promised to make Uni an earl if he succeeded, but the Icelanders would not listen to him and the entire journey was rather a sorry episode.

Dating from somewhat later, a legendary tale recounts how King Haraldur Bluetooth of Denmark, while on a military expedition in western Norway, had been planning to send warships to Iceland to capture the country. The King had been accused of ill-treating some shipwrecked travellers in Denmark, and was enraged at some scurrilous verses the Icelanders had made about him. First, the legend says, the King sent a wizard to the country to investigate its defences and landing places. The wizard changed himself into a whale and swam across the ocean to the coast of Iceland. But everywhere he tried to go ashore he was stopped by the guardian spirits of the country. In the east there was a dragon, in the north a vulture, in the west a terrible ox turned against him and in the south he was stopped by a giant with an iron club in his hand. These guardian spirits who forced the King to abandon his plans of conquest now decorate the coat of arms of the modern Icelandic Republic.

*Medival chalice, Patten and spoons.*

Some Norwegian kings begrudged the free and independent Icelandic republic and made intermittent attempts to increase their influence. King Ólafur Tryggvason tried hard to Christianize the Icelanders and interfered in their affairs in many ways. His efforts came to an abrupt end when he was killed in a battle early in his reign, in 1000. But the most determined attempts in this direction were made by King Ólafur Haraldsson, who immediately began to involve himself in Iceland's religious affairs as soon as he came to the throne of Norway in 1014. One of his actions was to proscribe deviations from true Christian faith, which he rewarded by sending timber for the church at Thingvellir. Some years later he sent an emissary, Thórarinn Nefjólfsson, to negotiate with the Icelandic chieftains. In a fine speech at parliament, Thórarinn said it would be both beneficial and wise for the Icelanders to secure the King's friendship and become subjects in his realm. But when he received no positive response he asked them to give the King, as a gesture of friendship, the little island of Grímsey, off the north coast. Many of the chieftains were willing to do so at first, until one of their number, who had not said a word before, rose and delivered an eloquent speech that convinced them against giving any piece of land away or allowing the Norwegian King to establish a base for his army in the country. The time of this King was cut short too, when the Norwegians revolted against him and killed him in a battle in 1030. Later, however, he became a national saint and was proclaimed an eternal King of Norway.

The Icelanders made a contract with King Ólafur Haraldsson around 1022, concerning the reciprocal duties, rights and privileges of Icelanders and Norwegians in each other's country, which was the first pact Iceland had ever made with a foreign state. Among other things, it allowed the Icelanders to take water and cut wood in the lands of the King when they came by ship to Norway.

# The Period of Peace

### *First Bishop at Skálholt*

*The episcopal sees of Skálholt and Hólar.*

It is customary to talk about the years from 1030 to 1118 as the period of peace. During this time the Christian religion put down lasting roots, bringing with it something of the Christian culture and making the Icelandic descendants of the Vikings participants in contemporary European civilization. The missionary bishops had worked diligently in the first decades of the eleventh century and some of them had kept schools where young men were taught to read and write, trained in Latin and other clerical learning, then ordained as priests to serve in the Church. Although this was of some help in a difficult situation, the shortage of priests remained acute. When the last missionary bishop, the Anglo-Saxon Rudolf, left in 1050, the chieftains and the rest of parliament agreed to ask the priest Ísleifur, son of Gissur the White, to go abroad and receive consecration as bishop.

Ísleifur had been educated at a famous school in Herford in Westphalia. His father had been one of the most influential leaders of Icelandic Christianity from its beginning. Ísleifur's family was rich and powerful and his maternal uncle was Skafti Thóroddsson, who was the lawspeaker in parliament from 1004 to 1030 and brought about many reforms in governmental as well as religious matters.

When Ísleifur sailed abroad he first visited the Archbishop of Bremen, who sent him to the Pope in Rome to ask dispensation to hold this high office, because he had earlier been married. On his way to Italy Ísleifur stopped at the court of the Holy Roman Emperor Henry III and presented him with a gift of a polar bear from Greenland. The delighted emperor asked many questions about these faraway lands, then gave him a letter of safe-conduct throughout his empire. The Pope received him well, too, and sent him back to the Archbishop of Bremen who consecrated him as bishop on Whitsunday in 1056.

*The episcopal seat of Skálholt in former times.*

Back home, Ísleifur set to work as a missionary bishop in Iceland and Greenland, because he was not consecrated to any particular diocese. As there was no episcopal see in the country at the time he settled at Skálholt in south Iceland which had earlier been his family farm. Alongside his other duties as bishop he established a theological seminary where he personally instructed a number of priests. Two of his students later became bishops, one in Iceland and one in Norway. Ísleifur nonetheless sent his own son Gissur abroad to study, then on to the Herford school where he had been himself. Bishop Ísleifur encountered some opposition in his work, but on the whole the Church and Christianity in Iceland strengthened in his time.

## Introduction of the Tithe

When Bishop Ísleifur died in 1080, learned and lay in parliament united to ask his son Gissur to take over. At first he was reluctant, until he extracted a promise from them to show him more obedience than they had his father. Gissur (1042–1118) was a very clever man and a born leader. A Norwegian king once said of him that three men could be made out of him: a king, a Viking chieftain or a bishop. Choosing the last option, he became bishop in his father's footsteps.

After his nomination Gissur visited the powerful Pope Gregory VII in Rome. At this time a struggle was going on between secular and spiritual leaders and the Pope was a bitter enemy of Emperor Henry IV. Since the Archbishop of Bremen, under whom the Icelandic Church then belonged, supported the emperor, the Pope sent Gissur to the Archbishop of Magdeburg to be consecrated.

On returning to take office, Gissur declared Skálholt, his family estate, the episcopal see for Iceland and endowed it with lands and other riches. Skálholt was originally intended to serve as a bishop's seat for as long as Christianity prevailed in the country, and in fact remained so for a very long time, almost to the end of the eighteenth century. In Skálholt, too, Gissur built a cathedral and strengthened the leadership and autonomy of the bishop and the Church in many ways.

His greatest achievement, however, was the introduction of the tithe in 1097, much earlier than in other Nordic countries. The tithe was the first general and proportionate tax levied in the country and amounted to 10% on income and 1% on property. This revenue was then equally divided among the bishop, churches, priests and, under a form of social relief, the poor. The tithe laid the foundation for the wealth and power of the church which continued to increase, for better or for worse, right up to the Reformation in 1550.

In his lifetime Gissur was highly respected and ruled not simply as bishop but virtually as king. This was an idyllic period, with mild and favourable farming weather, and peace and prosperity prevailed everywhere. The bishop's death in 1118 would leave a general feeling that much had taken a turn for the worse.

*The episcopal seat of Hólar in former times.*

## The Bishopric at Hólar

After Skálholt had been a bishopric for nearly half a century the people of north Iceland advocated the installation of a second bishop for themselves. Reasonably enough, they claimed there was less likelihood of the country ever being left without a bishop if there were two of them, but it is also possible that they felt too much money was being taken from north to south, and they preferred to see it kept locally. Bishop Gissur helped them to bring this about, and on his recommendation Jón Ögmundsson was elected as bishop for the north, a pious and learned priest who had studied abroad. He was consecrated at Lund in Denmark where the archbishop for the Nordic countries then sat. Half a century later, in 1152, the Icelandic Church came under the new archiepiscopal seat of Nidaros in Norway, where it remained until the Reformation.

Bishop Jón Ögmundsson had some difficulties in finding a convenient place for the episcopal seat in the north of Iceland, since none of the leading chieftains was willing to give up his estate for the purpose. Eventually the farmer at Hólar in Skagafjördur handed his land over to the new bishop. Hólar was made a permanent seat for the bishop and centre of this new

*Religious pictures.*

bishopric. The bishop of north Iceland sat there until 1801 when the office was abolished.

From the outset, Bishop Jón Ögmundsson proved himself to be a great church leader and brought about many reforms in his bishopric and the country in general. At Hólar he built a cathedral and a schoolhouse, and also established a cathedral school to educate priests, as in Skálholt. He hired learned teachers from abroad and it is clear that a strong cultural and religious awakening took place in his time. The cathedral school at Hólar was similar to other such institutions abroad at this time, with the seven liberal arts as its main subjects, and set the pattern for other schools in the country in medieval times.

But for all his good works for the Church, Jón Ögmundsson was inclined to asceticism and very austere in his manner. He preached against everything he found immoral and forbade dances and love songs. Another of his actions was to change the names of the days of the week so that they no longer recalled the heathen gods, as they did and still do in other Teutonic languages. Determined to establish a monastery in the country, he started to make some preparations but did not live long enough to realize that dream. He died in 1121. Twelve years later the monastery at Thingeyrar in the north came into being.

In connection with the establishment of the new bishopric in north Iceland, Bishop Gissur conducted a census of all taxpayers in the country. From that number, historians have estimated the total population to have been about 75–80,000 at this time.

# New Social Structure 1118–1220

## Consequences of the Tithe

The tithe of 1097 had great economic significance for the Church and changed the structure of the commonwealth radically. The Church became richer and the bishops more powerful, and the chieftains in the many and scattered principalities acquired more wealth, strengthened their position and increased their influence in many ways. They built churches on their estates and some of them were ordained as priests themselves or else hired priests to do the work, but in either case they received the tithe for church and priest and they also controlled the share which was meant for the poor. In this way they strengthened their position enormously, and the lower classes became dependent upon these masters as their tenants and workers.

This social system worked smoothly in the beginning while the numerous chieftains were roughly equal in power and wealth. But the balance of power was precarious and easily distorted, as would be seen later.

## The Art of Writing

In heathen times the Icelanders only knew the runic letters, with which they carved inscriptions in wood or stone. But the introduction of Christianity was accompanied by the Latin alphabet and books to use at church services. During the eleventh century the art of reading and writing spread considerably, and the law of the tithe was probably put into writing as soon as it was passed in 1097. The secular laws were first written down during the winter of 1117–18, and this late date could have been the result of opposition by chieftains who wanted to preserve the old custom of reciting the law at parliament; once the laws had been committed to writing, the lawspeaker no longer needed to know them by heart. This monumental corpus of law of the Saga Republic was later called Grágás or the Gray

Goose. Canon law or legislation for the Church was passed in parliament in 1123 and was probably written down at once. Afterwards, writing became quite a common activity. Among written works from the twelfth century were learned essays about the alphabet, Icelandic grammar and astronomy, historical works, chronologies, genealogies, homilies and prayer books, and from the beginning of the thirteenth century date the oldest Sagas, a history of the first bishops and several other texts. Such prolific output seems to prove the great number of highly educated men in the country at the time. The alphabet they used, with some modification, was derived from the English alphabet.

### The First Known Writer

Sæmundur Sigfússon (1056–1133) from Oddi was the first writer we know by name. He was highly educated and was said to have been the first person from any Nordic country to study in France. He lived as a priest and secular leader on his estate Oddi in south Iceland where he, too, established a school or seminary for priests. He became very influential both in worldly and ecclesiastical matters and was customarily consulted for advice if anything of importance was to be done. He is said to have written history books in Latin about the Norwegian kings and perhaps on other subjects. All his works were lost long ago, but later writers often quote him and his writings. A great number of folktales and legends have sprung up about his wisdom, especially in outwitting the devil, and he is constantly referred to as Sæmundur the Wise. In former times he was thought to be the author of the old Edda poems, but that cannot be the case.

*Sæmundur the Wise raises his Bible to smite the devil who is disguised as a seal, statue by Ásmundur Sveinsson.*

### The Classical Historian

Ari Thorgilsson (1067–1148) studied at Haukadalur near the great Geysir in south Iceland, where Teitur, son of bishop Ísleifur, ran a private school at that time. Later Ari served as priest in west Iceland, but little is

*Illuminated medieval manuscript.*

otherwise known about his private life. We do know for sure, however, that he wrote the first history of Iceland, the Íslendingabók or Book of Icelanders, in about 1130. This work, while rather short, contains an excellent summary of the main events in Icelandic history from the Age of Settlement down to the death of Bishop Gissur in 1118.

Ari Thorgilsson wrote his work at the wish of the bishops, Runólfur Thorláksson of Skálholt and Ketill Thorsteinsson of Hólar, and showed it to them and the priest Sæmundur the Wise, as he says himself in his preface. He compiled his history in Icelandic and is the first known writer in the vernacular. Ari probably wrote more than this single book, and is thought by some scholars to be the author of the original version of the Landnámabók, or Book of Settlements, from which extant versions derive. Lucid and conscious of the principles of objective historical scholarship, he is always known as Ari the Learned.

## The Monasteries

Jón Ögmundsson, the first bishop at Hólar, preached asceticism but did not live long enough to realize his plans for establishing a monastery. He had made some preparations and twelve years after his death, in 1133, the first Icelandic monastery was opened at Thingeyrar in the north. The monastic movement spread and altogether eleven cloisters – nine monasteries and two convents – were established around the country in the Catholic era. Some of these institutions were short-lived, but the great majority lasted until around 1550, when they were abolished under the Reformation. Besides Thingeyrar there were renowned monasteries at Mödruvellir in the north, the island Videy off Reykjavík, Helgafell in the west, Thykkvibaer in the south and the two nunneries at Kirkjubaer in the south and Reynistadur in the north. The cloisters were not only abodes for the religious-minded, but cultural and literary institutions as well. Historical works and Saga books were written in several of them, for instance at Thingeyrar, and many of them are known to have possessed good libraries. It can be taken for granted that knowledge of reading and writing spread from these institutions and farther afield.

*A seal from medieval times.*

The Icelandic monasteries belonged to the Benedictine or Augustinian orders. In the course of time they accumulated great riches and, as often happens where wealth is concerned, corruption and a delight in worldly living accompanied them. But on the whole, the cloisters did much good for the spiritual and intellectual life of the nation.

## Accumulation of Power

In the twelfth and early thirteenth centuries it was obvious that the social structure was changing rapidly. Alongside the growing wealth of the bishops, churches and cloisters, certain individuals and families gathered increasingly greater riches and power and began to behave just as they pleased, in defiance of the law and established social values. The chieftains not only kept their old principalities, but through gifts, marriages and inheritance acquired others. Properties became larger and power was concentrated in fewer and fewer hands.

This new upper class was fundamentally different from the ancient nobility, and the precarious balance of power was widely endangered. Many of these rich and powerful individuals thought more about their

*The door of Valthjófsstadur church, dating from about 1200.*

45

own interests than the welfare of the commonwealth. The resulting conflicts and even warfare gradually led to the dissolution of the old order.

## The Militant Church

*Head of a crozier.*

Originally, the Icelandic Church was a national institution; Christianity had been adopted by the ruling class and fused into the existing order. The ties between the Church and the upper class were further strengthened with the tithe of 1097, revenues from which had a marked impact on the finances of leading chieftains.

This state of affairs began to change in the twelfth century and even more sharply in the thirteenth, when the so-called militant Church took up the fight against all worldly powers. Its demand that the Church should be free and govern its own affairs without any interference by secular authorities was partly introduced to Iceland by Thorlákur Thórhallsson, bishop at Skálholt in 1178–93. He was well educated in England and France, and had returned to serve first as a priest and then as abbot in the Thykkvibaer Monastery, before being elected bishop. In that office he was devoutly religious and led a very ascetic life.

As bishop, Thorlákur actively challenged the worldly leaders who had built churches on their estates, preaching that they should give their estates to the Church and then receive them back as benefices. Initially the bishop had some success with his new policy, but the more powerful leaders fought against him and forced him to give up his demands.

With the support of the Archbishop of Nidaros, Bishop Thorlákur tried hard to reform morals among the chiefs and the common people. He achieved some success in these attempts and his preaching and ascetic views stirred interest and earned him widespread popular respect.

## Two Holy Men

The old Icelandic Church was no different from any

*The three holy bishops Gudmundur, Jón and Thorlákur, 15th-century antependium.*

other part of the Catholic Church in its emphasis on saints. Each church was dedicated to a particular saint, the most popular of whom included Mary, Nicholas, Peter and King Ólafur. Saints were worshipped in many ways and invoked in times of illness, need and distress, by giving offerings in their name to churches and other religious institutions.

For his piety and ascetic life, Bishop Thorlákur Thórhallsson of Skálholt was much admired by the common people in his lifetime. His church policy and fight against the nobles captured the popular imagination, despite his limited success in his campaign. After his death in 1193 people began to invoke this good bishop and believed a number of miracles had taken place in his name. In the 1198 Parliament his successor at Skálholt declared that people should be allowed to invoke him as a saint. His bones were unearthed and put into a sacred shrine in the cathedral, and the episcopal seat of Skálholt earned much money from endowments made in his name. But although he had been canonized in this way as a national saint, his name was not entered in the register of saints in Rome for a number of reasons; this was not done, in fact, until very recently, in 1984.

The rivalry which had earlier prompted the people of north Iceland to demand their own bishopric flared up once more with Thorlákur's elevation to sainthood, and the bishop, clergy and common people there were quick to discover manifestations that Jón Ögmunds-son, the first bishop at Hólar, had been a truly holy man and brought about his canonization too, in the year 1200. Thus the Icelandic Church had in a very short time acquired its two national saints, and people would invoke these holy and blessed bishops for centuries afterwards.

## A Troublesome Bishop

A priest, Gudmundur Arason, was elected bishop in the Hólar diocese in 1201. The leading chieftains in north Iceland had supported him, intending him to be their obedient tool, but their hopes were soon dashed. The new bishop was renowned for his sincere religious life and strong asceticism. Often he travelled around with vagrants and was followed by flocks of paupers. Among the many unusual things he did was to bless and consecrate well-water, dangerous roads and high birdcliffs. Many place names today still bear witness to this practice of the bishop's, including the main spring supplying drinking water for the capital, Reykjavík.

As bishop he was arbitrary and far from cooperative, claiming judiciary power over the clergy in accordance with the demands of the militant church at the time. When secular leaders denied him that right, great hostility and even warfare ensued between them and the bishop and his followers. In the end Bishop Gudmundur's enemies succeeded in driving him away from his episcopal seat at Hólar, and afterwards he largely lived like an outcast, roaming the countryside with his devoted flock.

This troublesome bishop put the law of God above worldly law and submitted all disputes with the ruling authorities to the judgement of the Archbishop of Nidaros in Norway. Such appeals to outside authorities to decide in internal quarrels and disputes opened the door for political interference from abroad, for secular leaders soon began to call upon the judgement of the King of Norway and obtain his support in their struggles for power in their own country.

Bishop Gudmundur Arason fought an unceasing war for the cause of the Holy Church, and lost. He died almost a prisoner at his episcopal see in 1237, after having spent most of his life like a prophet in the wilderness. But his sympathy for the poor and the scorned earned him great honour. The people called him Gudmundur the Good and looked upon him as a saint.

In the same year that Gudmundur Arason died, the office of the bishop of Skálholt fell vacant too. The Icelanders elected their candidates for these offices, but the Archbishop of Nidaros would not approve their nominations. Instead he consecrated two Norwegians to serve as bishops in Iceland, most probably both in order to ease the way for official papal policy and to consolidate the growing Norwegian influence. A little later, in 1253, it was decided in parliament that if secular and ecclesiastical law did not agree, the law of God should prevail. In the light of this ruling, Gudmundur Arason the Good can be said to have won a posthumous victory.

*Ecclesiastical painting from medieval times.*

# Dissolution of the Commonwealth 1220–1262

*Illumination from a medieval manuscript.*

## Struggle for Dominance

By the thirteenth century a few large families had gathered most of the political and economic power in the country into their hands. The equality of the aristocratic leaders had been disrupted and the old balance of power was thrown into disorder. A terrible struggle for power and warfare was the consequence.

At the same time, the monarchy strengthened in Norway, accompanied by growing interest in gaining sovereignty over all the countries which once had been settled from it. For this purpose the Norwegian King put pressure on certain leading Icelanders, playing them off against one another as if in a game of chess. In his efforts he was greatly helped by the Church and especially by the Archbishop of Nidaros under whom the Icelandic Church belonged.

Ecclesiastical and royal ambition were not the only forces at work, for the Icelanders were no longer self-sufficient in ships and depended heavily on Norway for export and import. Norwegian merchants, mostly from Bergen which was the centre for the Iceland trade, supported the king in his endeavour to gain more power in Iceland and felt it was in their own interest to help him to that end.

## Snorri Sturluson (1179–1241)

The Sturlungar family from west Iceland was the most influential in this period, and for a long time Snorri Sturluson, the great historian, was its leading chieftain. In effect he virtually ruled the country from about 1220 to 1235. He had been brought up at the estate of Oddi in south Iceland by the rich, cultivated and at that time very powerful family there, and gained not only an excellent education but also support which would help him make his own way in life. Snorri later proved to be a clever negotiator and shrewd politician, but not much of a military leader. Despite great abilities in many fields, his main weaknesses were avarice and a tendency to be unscrupulous, even towards his relatives and own children. With his first wife he acquired power and riches, but he divorced her to gain control of still more wealth with his second wife. He married his daughters off to leading men in other noble families and, short-lived as these marriages proved to be, they nonetheless brought him wealth and power far and wide in Iceland.

Snorri Sturluson served twice as the lawspeaker or president of the general assembly, in 1215–18 and again in 1222–31. In 1218–20 he stayed in Norway, where he settled a serious dispute and fighting which had broken out between some Icelandic chieftains and Norwegian merchants. In Norway at this time King Hákon Hákonarson had come to power, but the country was governed for the most part by the mighty earl Skúli Bárdarson in the name of his teenage royal son-in-law. Earl Skúli was one of the many powerful Norwegians at the time who were enraged by the hardships and losses suffered by some of their merchants in Iceland, and was on the verge of sending a marine expedition to take revenge and possibly bring the country under the King of Norway. But Snorri Sturluson arrived in time to stop this. Instead of military action, he promised to guarantee the merchants peace and to promote the King's cause in Iceland. It is very likely that he also promised to bring the country under the King's rule in a peaceful manner – at least, that is what many of his contemporaries claimed. Snorri Sturluson became a close friend of the earl and a retainer of the King before sailing back to Iceland laden with gifts on board a ship which the earl had given him. Back home again, Snorri Sturluson did nothing to promote Norwegian influence in Iceland or plead the King's cause among his countrymen, although the merchants were able to go about their businesses in peace from then on.

*Iceland's greatest historian, Snorri Sturluson – statue by Gustav Wigeland, a gift from Norway to Iceland.*

## The Battle of Örlygsstadir

King Hákon of Norway seems to have been determined to bring Iceland under his rule. Soon realizing
that Snorri Sturluson would not do for that purpose,
he befriended Snorri's nephew, Sturla Sighvatsson,
made him a retainer of his court and sent him back to
Iceland as his representative in 1235. Sturla was more
of a military figure than his uncle Snorri, and at once
started a civil war in the country which lasted peri-
odically until the bitter end of the old republic in
1262.

But the rule of Sturla Sighvatsson did not last long.
He tyrannized over his opponents but never quite
managed to subdue them. Their main leaders were
Gissur Thorvaldsson, the head of the southern Haukadalur family, and Kolbeinn Arnórsson from the north.
These two chieftains managed to gather great forces
and kill Sturla himself, his father, three of his brothers
and a number of other followers in the fateful battle of
Örlygsstadir in 1238, when the once powerful Sturlungar family was nearly destroyed.

## The Slaying of Snorri Sturluson

As victors, Gissur Thorvaldsson and Kolbeinn Arnórsson assumed virtual control of Iceland. Gissur had
formerly stayed in Norway, where the King had made
him, too, his retainer and friend.

Snorri Sturluson was on one of his many visits to
earl Skúli Bárdarson when he heard the news of the
Örlygsstadir battle where so many of his kinsmen had
been killed, and asked permission to sail back home
to take care of his affairs and possessions. The King
refused, invoking the right he enjoyed over his retainers, but the Earl allowed him to leave.

Shortly afterwards Skúli Bárdarson revolted against
his son-in-law, the King, with the aim of taking all
power in Norway into his own hands, but was killed
in one of the battles which ensued. Furious at this act
of treason, the King thought his disobedient retainer
Snorri Sturluson must also have been implicated in

*Medieval weapons.*

the conspiracy. He promptly sent orders to Gissur Thorvaldsson either to send Snorri back to Norway or kill him. Gissur, who had once been married to one of Snorri's daughters, seems not to have even entertained the thought of sending him abroad, but took a band of men to Snorri's home at Reykholt in west Iceland and killed this great historian and writer on a dark September night in 1241.

## Gissur and Thórdur

Gissur Thorvaldsson set off for Norway in 1242 to visit King Hákon, leaving his ally Kolbeinn Arnórsson in Iceland as the leading chieftain. But about the same time Thórdur Sighvatsson, the only surviving brother of Sturla Sighvatsson, returned from Norway where he too had become a retainer of the King, who was now sending him to Iceland for the purpose of bringing the country under his rule. At first Thórdur was met with great suspicion and hostility, but he proved to be a clever and noble leader and acquired power over a great deal of the country in a fairly peaceful way. However, he suffered some losses in a great sea battle against Kolbeinn Arnórsson in 1244, then won another on land at Haugsnes two years later, although without resolving the struggle for power completely.

After the death of Kolbeinn Arnórsson, Gissur and Thórdur found themselves more or less equal in strength and decided that, since they were both courtiers of the Norwegian King, they would ask him to decide which of them should rule the country. They arrived in 1247, in the midst of great festivities when King Hákon was being formally crowned by Cardinal William of Sabina and given the blessing of the Church. When the King introduced the Icelanders to the cardinal and told him about the state of affairs on their distant island, the cardinal replied that it was most improper for a country to deviate from the established order elsewhere in the world, by not belonging to any king. He also deemed Thórdur Sighvatsson's cause to be better than Gissur's. King Hákon was of the same opinion and sent Thórdur back to Iceland to bring the country under his rule for good.

Thórdur reigned peacefully in Iceland, enjoying almost absolute power from 1247 to 1250. But when the Norwegian bishop at Hólar complained that he did not plead the King's cause properly, Thórdur was obliged to go back to Norway to explain the situation. He was not allowed to resume power, nor to return, and stayed in Norway until his death in 1256.

### The Flames at Flugumýri

King Hákon did not give up his attempts to gain control of Iceland. In 1252 he sent Gissur Thorvaldsson back in his name to finish the work. Gissur immediately gained control of the south and north quarters, but the men Thórdur Sighvatsson had left in office as his deputies were not happy. They gathered great forces and during a wedding celebration in 1253 they attacked Gissur's manor farm at Flugumýri in north Iceland, burnt down the houses and killed his wife, all three sons and a number of other people. Gissur himself escaped in a miraculous way by hiding in a tub of sour whey until his enemies had gone.

Gissur Thorvaldsson took revenge as best he could and killed many of his enemies, but since he was not thought loyal enough to the King either, he too had to go to Norway in 1254. After that the King sent his own countrymen to join the bishops in bringing Iceland under his rule, and they helped the King score his best success so far in this aim when certain local chieftains agreed to pay taxes to him.

## The Final Phase

*A Medieval spear.*

After the death of Thórdur Sighvatsson, King Hákon dispatched yet another member of the Sturlungar family to Iceland: Thorgils Bödvarsson, who had earlier served as his retainer. Thorgils governed some of the districts Thórdur Sighvatsson had ruled over, until he was treacherously killed in 1258. By then, all the leading Icelanders whom the King had appointed as his retainers and used for his own ends were dead, except Gissur Thorvaldsson. With no other hope to rely on, the King gave him the title of earl, a coat of arms and a trumpet in 1258, whereupon Gissur took power in both the south and north of the country.

Yet Gissur did not do anything to bring the country under the King. In all likelihood he only wanted to establish his own earldom in Iceland as a free and independent state with the support of the King of Norway. But if this was his intention, it soon became clear that the King thought otherwise. He sent over a number of his closest agents, who with the backing of the bishops pressed Gissur to keep his promises about delivering sovereignty and taxation into Norwegian hands. In 1262 these royal representatives manipulated Gissur into making the leading chieftains in parliament swear oaths of allegiance to the King, and those who were absent then were forced to do so over the next two years. Since the Greenlanders had already acknowledged Norwegian sovereignty in 1261, the King had succeeded in his aims.

This final move in a long and complex series of manoeuvres saw the Icelanders finally lose their independence in 1262 and become subjects of the King of Norway. In fact, they were not supposed to have anything in common with Norway except the King, on the basis of personal union through him with that country. But events turned out differently and Iceland very soon became a tributary country of Norway.

The old aristocratic republic in Iceland had lasted

for 332 years, from 930 to 1262. Its main weakness had been that it had no executive power to maintain law and order. During the struggle for supremacy in the thirteenth century none of the leading Icelandic chieftains was strong enough to establish the requisite power, and therefore they sought it from abroad. King Hákon of Norway exploited the situation to gain power in Iceland, with the help of these local chieftains and with the Church, where he had a firm ally in the Archbishop of Nidaros. For some decades only Norwegian bishops were sent to Iceland, but after the country had lost its independence Icelandic bishops took over again.

It was a combination of circumstances which brought the decline and fall of the old Icelandic republic, but we should remember that the Icelandic people were never conquered at all.

## The Old Treaty

In 1262 the Icelanders made a treaty with the King of Norway which is often called The Old Treaty. Under it they acknowledged the King as their sovereign and promised to pay him a yearly tax in perpetuity, in return for a promise from him to maintain peace and Icelandic law in the country. Terms for shipping and trade were also stipulated, whereby six ships were to bring goods from Norway to Iceland each summer for the following two years, and thereafter as many as was thought fit. There were clauses leaving inheritance and other rights of Icelanders in Norway unaffected, while the earl was established as governor of Iceland as long as he remained loyal to the King and kept peace with the Icelanders.

Finally, the Icelanders obliged themselves and their heirs to respect this treaty towards the King and his heirs, as long as they did likewise; if, in the opinion of "the best men", they failed to do so, the Icelanders would no longer be subject to its provisions.

This treaty, and especially this final clause, was frequently quoted by the Icelanders in their efforts to preserve their rights through the ages, and even in their campaign for freedom and independence in the nineteenth century.

## *Literary Greatness*

*Medieval manuscript and a modern passport.*

Although it may sound like a contradiction in the light of all this upheaval, it is nevertheless a fact that cultural and literary life in medieval Iceland rose to unparalleled heights in the thirteenth century. In the midst of political dissolution, a merciless civil war, general enmity and evil deeds of all kinds, most of the greatest sagas were written, such as Egils saga, Laxdaela saga, Njáls saga and a number of other remarkable works which will always rank highly in world literature. We do not know the authors of these sagas, for they never put their names to them – perhaps because they felt they only were recording what they had heard in oral tradition from older generations.

More is known, however, about the authors of some historical works. For instance we know that Karl Jónsson wrote a life of King Sverrir Sigurdsson of Norway, and that Snorri Sturluson wrote the Younger Edda, about poetry and pagan mythology. Snorri also wrote a monumental historical work about the Norwegian kings, the Heimskringla, and perhaps some sagas too. His nephew, Sturla Thórdarson, wrote an important contemporary history of Iceland and works about King Hákon Hákonarson of Norway and his son Magnús the Reformer. Some other descendants of the gifted Sturlungar family were also known as great poets and writers.

The manuscripts of the sagas, histories, poetry and other literature of medieval times were written on specially treated calf-skin parchments called vellum, because paper was not introduced to Iceland until the fifteenth century or even later. Although many of these old manuscripts have been lost in the course of time, others have been preserved right up to the present day and form precious treasures in the Icelandic cultural heritage.

# Under Foreign Rule

## The Turning-Point

The year 1262 marks the major turning-point in the history of Iceland, when the long and often dark ages of foreign rule began which were to last in one form or other until the proclamation of the new republic in 1944, for 682 years in all. Probably this change in government was not considered particularly remarkable at the time, and seen rather as a way to be allowed to live in peace after long and bitter civil strife. In the literature, however, we read about evil dreams and sinister forebodings at the loss of the old freedom and independence.

Much else began to change, too, especially in the cultural life of the nation. Saga writing ebbed out for the most part in the fourteenth century, and other literary genres changed and slowly declined. But the most striking feature of the new age was the steadily growing power of the King and his representatives, on the one hand, and of the Church on the other. The King, for instance, now began to acquire land in Iceland. The first real estates he claimed were several great farms formerly belonging to Snorri Sturluson, including the farm of Bessastadir south of Reykjavík, which was later made the headquarters of the royal governors and other officers and served as such for many centuries. In former times this gave Bessastadir a rather shady reputation in the minds of many people, but this has changed since it was made the official presidential residence under the new Republic of Iceland.

## Earldom Abolished

Gissur Thorvaldsson reigned as earl or viceroy to the end of his life in 1268. Under his rule, peace was restored for the most part in the country. Only the leading chieftains of the Oddi estate in the south refused to accept the earl's supremacy and revolted against him. After some military clashes, both sides agreed to negotiate about their dispute. Gissur promptly betrayed his opponents, captured their leader, Thórdur Andrésson, and had him beheaded in 1264. Afterwards he no longer encountered any serious resistance from secular leaders, but in many ways he had to bow to the growing power of the Church and ecclesiastical law.

Gissur's power base was confined to the south and north quarters and he never gained control of the whole country. The King had other representatives in the east and west and probably did not trust the earl completely. Earl Gissur was a somewhat tragic figure. None of the worldly fame or power that had been the motivating force in his life could compensate for the loss of his wife and three sons that had been one of its consequences. Perhaps he did not find much purpose in life as it was, for he was planning to retire from office and seek peace for his soul in a monastery when he was taken ill and died in 1268, only fifty-nine years old. Before he passed on, he made a gift for the good of his soul of a large estate where a nunnery was later established.

After Gissur's death the earldom remained vacant and some years later it was officially abolished. While Gissur lived no great governmental changes were made, but the King was to use his complete executive power to introduce radical reforms over the next few decades.

## New Codes of Law

King Hákon of Norway died in 1263 and his son, Magnús Hákonarson, succeeded him and reigned until his death in 1280. King Magnús was a great law-maker and drew up separate new codes of law for both Norway and Iceland, and became known as Magnús the Reformer. The King engaged some Icelanders to work with him on this new code and it was partly based on the law of the old republic, although not sufficiently in their opinion. The first lawbook for Iceland was issued in 1271, but only partly accepted by the

*Illumiation from a medieval manuscript.*

Icelandic parliament. Many new laws were added, including the formal prohibition of the blood-feud or vendetta which had been practised from the earliest times.

Because of parliamentary and popular reluctance to accept it, the first lawbook was revised and issued again in 1280, when the greater part of it was endorsed and would remain in effect for centuries. The Icelandic parliament still had extensive legislative power, in theory at least, but the King could make laws too and the difference between his legislative powers and those of parliament was not clearly defined.

A new code of canonical law was also written and accepted in 1275 in the Skálholt diocese, in which the difference between ecclesiastical and secular power was defined more clearly, and considerably in favour of the Church.

### Feudalism of the Church

Árni Thorláksson was bishop in Skálholt from 1269 to 1298. He had been elected by the cathedral chapter in Nidaros, as had been the custom since 1238, and was backed by the Archbishop there. As a true representative of the international Church and the Pope, he at once began a campaign to rule over all estates and other possessions where churches had been built, and after a long and hard dispute he succeeded, with the support of both the Archbishop and the King. By this action the Church amassed great riches in the form of lands. Freeholders who had previously lived on these farms now became tenants of the Church and a definite form of feudalism was introduced.

The new code of Church law gave the bishops much more authority, for instance full judiciary power in all clerical matters, which meant that they could impose fines for a number of offences, enforced with the threat of excommunication and interdiction. Among other things, the bishops now demanded celibacy of the servants of the Church. This was something new in Iceland and was not taken very seriously in the beginning, but it proved to be a useful weapon in the hands of the bishops in the future.

## A Country to Let

Through family connections with the royal house of Norway, Iceland came under the king of Sweden for a few decades in the fourteenth century. Although this state of affairs did not last long, it became a custom during this period to lease Iceland for a fixed sum. Leaseholders usually had the country for a three-year period at a time and naturally squeezed as much money out of the bargain as they possibly could, in many cases through ill treatment dispensed by ruthless governors.

Now and again there were revolts against such tyrants, as happened in 1361 when the governor of that time, Smidur Andrésson, rode with a party of attendants across the highlands to north Iceland to harass and subdue the farmers there. But the people were on their guard and managed to gather forces, killing the governor and a number of his followers in the ensuing battle. This and similar events were immortalized in legends and poetry, and were considered good and noble deeds.

## The Kalmar Union

King Hákon VI of Norway and Iceland married a Danish princess, Margaret, the daughter of King Valdemar of Denmark. When King Valdemar died in 1375 the six-year-old son of Margaret and Hákon, Oluf by name, ascended to the Danish throne. The country was governed in his name, however, by his wily mother. Five years later, in 1380, his father, King Hákon of Norway and Iceland, died too, and this young boy inherited all his countries. But since he was still too young for the task, these countries were ruled by his mother as well. The Icelanders swore oaths of allegiance to the young Oluf as their King in 1383, marking the beginning of long-lasting ties between Iceland, Norway and Denmark.

King Oluf Hákonarson came of age in 1385, but died only two years later at the age of seventeen. With this his mother seemed to lose her power base, but with the support of both the Church and the nobility she managed to reign on as "the mighty lady and right master" in Denmark, Norway and all the tributary countries like Iceland, Greenland, the Faroe Islands, Shetland and the Orkneys. In 1397 this powerful Queen chose her relative, Eric of Pommern, as her heir. Since the Swedes had revolted against their King, Albrecht of Mecklenburg, and chosen her to rule them too, Eric of Pommern was duly crowned as their King in 1397. During the coronation, at the town of Kalmar in Sweden, the Queen declared a union of all the Nordic countries, under her rule: the Kalmar Union, which was intended as a perpetual buffer against German expansion. In fact it was a rather loose alliance, which Sweden repeatedly left and joined again until it eventually left to establish its own royal house under Gustav Vasa in 1523. Margaret ruled her countries firmly until she died in 1412, but King Eric was not as successful. In the end he was driven from the throne and ended his life as a pirate in the Baltic Sea.

## The Great Plague (Black Death)

The Great Plague or Black Death raged in Norway, as in most countries in Europe, from about 1349 to 1350. Fatalities were incredible, and some sources estimate that half or even two thirds of the population were lost. At this time the plague did not reach Iceland because there was no shipping from abroad; but about half a century later, in 1402–04, the same or a similar plague raged there, killing rich and poor alike in huge numbers. It is impossible to say precisely how many died, but the victims have been estimated at between one third and one half of the population. There were many tragic stories from this time: the plague spread so fast that of fifteen people who went to a funeral on one occasion, only four or five returned.

*Dying people in The Great Plague.*

This devastating plague had various consequences. With so few people left, a large number of farms fell into disuse, and more still came under the Church as gifts from dying people. Prices of land fell and rent stayed low for a long time afterwards, making it easier for poor people to acquire land and establish themselves as farmers, while the sharp drop in the working population forced wages to rise. Lax morality and lawlessness of various kinds followed, and in many senses the plague caused a cultural breakdown; for instance, there are relatively few written sources from this time because literary activities stopped for the most part.

It is quite certain that the Icelandic nation took a very long time to recover from this calamity, even though the population soon began to grow again. And this was not the only shock of this kind in the fifteenth century, because in 1494–95 a new wave of plague raged with similar consequences as the Black Death, although this epidemic never reached the fjords in the northwest corner of the country.

## The English Century

In the fifteenth century Icelandic stockfish had become very valuable and was in great demand in many countries. Fish took over from the old homespun wool-

*Seabattle between German and English ships off Iceland.*

len cloth which had been Iceland's main export article. Norwegian merchants had handled the Iceland trade for a long time, but in the fifteenth century the German merchants of the Hanseatic League took an increasing share. They set up many trading posts in Norway, making Bergen on its west coast their headquarters. In Iceland, however, it has become customary to talk about the period as the English Century, because seamen from England began to fish in the rich Icelandic waters at that time. Initially the English only sent a few ships to Iceland, but their number increased from year to year to reach about 150 in 1428. With all this shipping, the Norwegian, or rather German, merchants lost their monopoly on the Iceland trade, because the English not only fished but carried on considerable trade at the same time. They even hired a number of people to work for them, and paid well. For a long time there were strong English influences in Iceland and even some emigration to England. The English established several fishing stations in Iceland, the biggest being on the Westman Islands, off the south coast.

Disapproving of the English presence in Iceland, the Danish King tried hard to oust them, helped in his endeavours by German seamen and merchants of the Hanseatic League which by this time had largely taken over the Iceland trade. Occasional battles were fought between these rivals, but the English went on with their business and generally traded peacefully with the Icelanders. In some instances, however, the Icelanders had to defend themselves and even fight back. In one such skirmish, in north Iceland in 1431, there were heavy casualties. An Englishman, John Williamson Craxton, had been appointed as bishop to the Hólar see about the same time, and although he supported his countrymen and promoted the English cause in Iceland for a while, he was eventually forced to give up and leave the country.

A rich Icelander, Björn Thorleifsson, whom the King had made one of his governors, tried to stop the English, but was killed in a battle in west Iceland in 1467. Then his belligerent wife, Ólöf Loftsdóttir, said the famous words: "Let us not cry for my husband, Björn, but gather troops and take revenge." This she did and had many of the English killed, and took others as prisoners and kept them as slaves on her estate of Skard.

After protracted struggles and several "cod wars" between the Danes and the English, an agreement was reached in 1490, whereby the English were allowed to fish and trade in Iceland if they applied for permits to do so. This arrangement worked at first, but the treaty was broken and eventually the settlement fell through. All the same, it still took a long time for the Danes and their German allies to get rid of the English, who only abandoned their last stronghold, on the Westman Islands, in 1558. Control of the Iceland trade then moved completely into the hands of the Danes, although the Germans continued to handle it for some time afterwards.

## Acts of Violence

Corruption was rife within the Church in the fourteenth and fifteenth centuries, and even high offices were for sale. Jón Gerreksson, a Dane and a great favourite of Eric of Pommern at the time of the Kalmar Union, had won or bought the office of Archbishop of Uppsala in Sweden. Soon becoming involved in troubles, he was driven out of this office and the country by the Swedes, so the King appointed him bishop of Skálholt, possibly with the aim of using him against the English who were then very influential in Iceland. The bishop took a number of foreign soldiers with him, and he and his men at once started to harass people in Iceland and commit outrages.

When the leader of the bishop's bodyguard was rejected by a young noblewoman he had proposed to, he attacked her family and killed her brother in a fit of rage. The young lady narrowly escaped and swore she would marry the man who would take revenge for this crime. The bishop had already made many enemies among the men he had been fighting. Some had been taken prisoner and subjected to ill treatment, and when they finally escaped from captivity they gathered troops and attacked the bishop and his followers at Skálholt. After some fighting the Icelanders overpowered the bishop, dragged him from the cathedral, put him in a sack and drowned him in a nearby river. Most of his men were killed too, although some managed to escape on an English ship which they had captured.

The lawlessness of these times was such that nobody seems to have had to answer for this bloody act of violence, which happened in 1433, shortly before King Eric of Pommern was forced to leave his throne. But the young lady kept her word, and married one of the leaders of this action against the bishop of Skálholt.

### Subsistence and Survival

Farming continued to be the main form of subsistence, as it had been from the beginning. Cattle and sheep were most commonly reared, for meat, milk, wool, leather and hides. There were some other animals too, such as pigs, goats, poultry and horses. Haymaking took place in the summertime, and there was also some gardening and growing of grain, mostly barley because of the unsuitability of the climate for other crops of that sort. Besides farming there was always plenty of fishing. When rising demand for stockfish put prices up, some farmers on the coast earned a handsome living as outfitters of fishing boats. A new wealthy class thereby grew up in some parts of the south and southwest of the country, although both the King and the Church took their share of these new-found riches before long. The main staples of the common diet were meat, fish and dairy products of various kinds. Grain had to be imported for the most part and bread, being expensive, was not much used. Many other necessities also had to be imported, like salt, iron, timber, utensils of many kinds, fine clothes and countless other articles. Nonetheless, ordinary people tried to be as self-sufficient as they could, preserving their food for long periods by such means as smoking or drying meat and fish and curdling milk products.

Driftwood was widely used instead of imported timber, and most houses were built with turf and stone walls. The old birch forests were relentlessly exploited for implements and buildings and still more for firewood and charcoal, and destroyed to a great extent. Iron and other metals were rare and expensive because they had to be brought in from abroad, but to make tools and implements for everyday use the people had their home-made bog iron. Clothes were largely home-made from wool, and shoes were made of sheepskin and hides.

The struggle for basic survival was often hard, because of the cold climate and spells of bad weather. Terrible volcanic eruptions occurred from time to time, some of them inflicting great damage. Sometimes polar ice would drift down from the north and up to the coast, which compounded the problem of poor pastures, crop failures and generally meagre land. The population was harassed by plagues and all manner of epidemics that sometimes came close to rivalling the infamous Black Death of 1402–04 in casualties: smallpox, measles and a number of other diseases took intermittent toll of hundreds and thousands of lives. Under such conditions the size of the population fluctuated sharply. It has been estimated as averaging between 40,000 and 60,000 in the early fifteenth century.

# The Reformation of 1550

*Martin Luther.*

*King Christian III.*

## *Approaching Protestantism*

Martin Luther started the Reformation movement in Germany in 1517 with his ninety-five theses against abuses within the Catholic Church. One of the objects of his protests was the letters of indulgence which the Pope had for sale in many countries, and had even reached as far as Iceland, for we read that stockfish was shipped away in payment for remission of sins. Lutheranism or Protestantism spread rapidly in North Germany and soon reached the Scandinavian countries. New ideas spread much faster at this time with the recent introduction of the art of printing.

King Christian II of Denmark and his Union army were driven out of Sweden in 1523 by a mass revolt after his massacre of the Swedish nobility three years earlier. Leaving the Kalmar Union for good, the Swedes established their own national kingdom with Gustav Ericson Vasa on the throne. He introduced the Lutheran faith to Sweden in 1527 and thereby gained control over the great riches of the Church.

The subjects of Christian II in Denmark revolted against him, too, and replaced him with his uncle, Frederick II, on whose death in 1533 civil war broke out. Christian II, who was married to the sister of the Holy Roman Emperor Charles V, tried hard to regain the throne, but when he was finally defeated after years of fighting and imprisoned for the rest of his life, his kinsman Christian III succeeded to it. During these hard times Christian II was always in great need of money, and even tried to mortgage or sell both Iceland and the Faroe Islands to Henry VIII of England to finance his warfare, but the latter would not buy them. Christian III became King in 1536 and in the same year he formally established the Lutheran Church in Denmark, Norway and the Faroe Islands. Because of special circumstances the Icelanders were able to adhere to the old faith a little longer. The new church ordinance of Christian III meant that the respective sovereign replaced the Pope as head of the Church, and that all possessions of both the Church and the monasteries came under his control. It is not surprising that contemporary sovereigns should have been attracted to the Lutheran faith, for the increased power and wealth it brought them, irrespective of the doctrines on which it was founded.

### The Last Catholic Bishops

*Episcopal seal.*

The last Catholic bishops in Iceland were Ögmundur Pálsson in the Skálholt diocese and Jón Arason at Hólar. They were both strong and powerful leaders, eager to amass as much wealth for the Church and themselves as they possibly could. Originally they had been bitter enemies because Ögmundur had wanted another candidate for the episcopal see of Hólar. But with the approach of Lutheranism they had found a common cause as allies against it. While civil war raged in Denmark and nobody really knew who was king, these Icelandic bishops had acted in the name of the Norwegian state council as governors in their country, wielding both ecclesiastical and secular power for some years. The new faith found its way to Iceland fairly quickly through the many Hanseatic merchants stationed there. In Hafnarfjördur, south of Reykjavík, these merchants even had their own Lutheran church. Owing to German trade connections, which were mostly with Hamburg, a number of young Icelanders went to study in Germany and became acquainted with the new faith. Many of them embraced its teachings and took them back home with them. As a result, in a relatively short time, a strong group of adherents of the Lutheran creed had grown up in south Iceland. One of them was Oddur Gottskálksson, who translated the New Testament into Icelandic, working secretly at this task in Skálholt behind the back of the strictly Catholic bishop. His translation, printed and published in Denmark in 1540, was the first book ever printed in the Icelandic language.

The followers of the new faith worked quietly for their cause at first, but after the introduction of Luther-

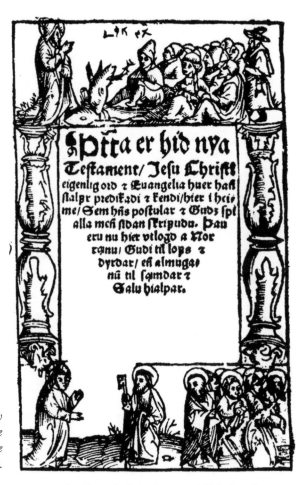

*Title page of the 1540 New Testament in Icelandic, the first book printed in the vernacular.*

anism in the Danish kingdom in 1537 they began to speak more openly about it.

## Lutheranism in the South

When the official announcement of the new Church ordinance in the Danish Kingdom reached Iceland in 1538, the bishop and his clergy in the Skálholt diocese rose against it, denouncing it as heresy. The next year the bishop had a letter read in all churches of his diocese in which he threatened excommunication for anybody who listened to the heresies of the German monk. The same year, 1539, the King sent a new governor to Iceland, Klaus von Mervitz, with a mandate to clear the way for the Reformation and take over some of the Church's possessions. He seized the Videy monastery with the help of his sheriff, Dietrich of Minden, and his soldiers. They drove the monks away heavy-handedly and seized all the possessions in the name of the King, for which the old bishop of Skálholt promptly excommunicated them. Later the same summer when the sheriff and his band of men were on their way to take over some other monasteries, they stopped at Skálholt and treated the bishop badly despite his warnings not to do so. The bishop's friends and supporters then gathered forces from the surrounding districts and attacked and killed Dietrich and all his men.

Bishop Ögmundur was by now old and nearly blind. He had made an arrangement for his favourite, Gissur Einarsson, to be elected as his successor in Skálholt. Gissur was a clever and able man, but as an adherent of Protestantism he played a double game with his benefactor who thought he was a staunch Catholic. When Gissur arrived in Copenhagen, the King had heard about the slaying of his men at Skálholt and put the blame on the old bishop. Sent back to Iceland by the furious King without being consecrated, Gissur tried hard to work for the new Church ordinance, but his message was roundly denounced in the parliament of 1540. The same parliament also acquitted of any crime all those involved in killing the sheriff and his soldiers at Skálholt.

Bishop Jón Arason and his clergy in the north wrote a letter to the King asking his dispensation to keep their old faith and remain in the Catholic Church, and also requesting his permission to emigrate with their possessions to some other country if he would not grant this. The King replied by sending a naval expedition to Iceland the following summer which, with the support of Gissur Einarsson, used brute force to subdue all resistance. Bishop Ögmundur was betrayed, taken prisoner and sent to Denmark, where he died in custody in 1542. The Danish representatives of the King had the new Church ordinance accepted for the Skálholt diocese in parliament in 1541, and Gissur Einarsson was consecrated a year later.

As bishop, Gissur Einarsson encountered enormous difficulties with so few Lutheran clergymen to serve in the new Church. He had trouble, too, in combatting the old belief in holy men and relics, but did his best to eradicate all such abuses of the new ordinance. One of his actions was to break down a holy cross in the neighbourhood of Skálholt. On his way back home from this deed he was taken ill and died shortly afterwards, which the people said was a token of God's punishment. Gissur Einarsson ruled as bishop in Skálholt from 1542 until his death in 1548. He seems to have been on good terms with Jón Arason, the Catholic bishop of the north, and they both kept the peace. In his own diocese, Gissur did his best to establish the new faith and was partly successful in his mission.

### The Lost Cause of Jón Arason

After the Lutheran Church had been introduced and accepted in the Skálholt diocese, Jón Arason at Hólar was the last Catholic bishop left in all the Nordic countries. When Gissur Einarsson died in 1548 the Protestant clergy chose Marteinn Einarsson as his successor in Skálholt. Then Jón Arason appeared on the scene and arranged for a Catholic priest to be elected to the same office. He also wrote letters to the Pope and the Emperor, asking them for support, for which the King accused him of high treason and declared him an outlaw. In Copenhagen nothing was done with the Catholic priest, but Marteinn Einarsson received his consecration and returned to take up his episcopal see in 1549.

Jón Arason prepared to defend himself and fight for his religion if necessary, even going so far as to fortify his episcopal see at Hólar. He managed to take Bishop Marteinn prisoner and kept him in custody at Hólar, then rode with a band of armed men to parliament where he was given consent to rule the Skálholt diocese as well as his own. He took Skálholt by force

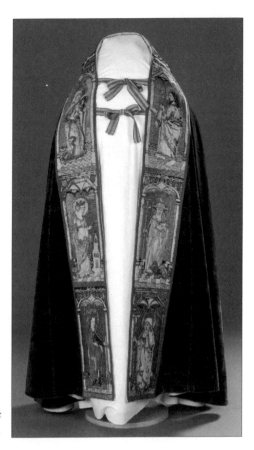

*Bishop Jón Arason's robe.*

and did his utmost to purge it of the new teaching, then restored the monastery on Videy. Bishop Jón was very proud of these deeds and wrote a poem about them, for he was one of the most accomplished poets of his time.

Dadi Gudmundsson, a rich man from west Iceland who served in many high offices, was an adherent of the Lutheran faith and very loyal to the King, who entrusted him to take Bishop Jón Arason prisoner. The bishop acted promptly and issued a summons on Dadi for various offences, then rode with a band of armed men to the west of Iceland to subdue him, but was attacked by his superior forces. After this battle in autumn 1550, the bishop was taken prisoner together with two of his sons, Ari and Björn. He also had other children with his mistress Helga Sigurdardóttir.

The bishop and his sons were taken to Skálholt to be kept prisoner until the 1551 parliament would determine their fate. Some Danish officials and Icelanders who were appointed to guard them were very afraid that men from the north would come to rescue their leaders, and in their anxiety one of the guards declared that "the axe and the earth would keep them best". It was soon decided, after repeating former charges against them, to put all three of them to death. On November 7, 1550, they were beheaded at Skálholt.

News of these executions did not reach Copenhagen until the next summer, when the King had already sent a large military expedition to the north of Iceland. With the rebels against him dead by then, his men made do with extracting oaths of allegiance to the King and approval for his church ordinance from representatives of the people in the diocese. The Reformation had gone into force all over the country.

After the bishop was beheaded, however, a group from north Iceland killed all the Danes who had had anything to do with the execution, and another went to Skálholt to fetch the bodies of the bishop and his sons back to Hólar for burial. Many legends are connected with the transportation of his relics and with the name of Jón Arason and his battle for his faith and country.

# Consequences of the Reformation

## A Cultural Shock

Jón Arason, the last Catholic bishop, died a martyr for his faith, and, to a certain degree, for the freedom of his countrymen. Although some people at that time were genuine adherents of Lutheranism, and others were indifferent or only interested in stopping the greed and abuses of the Catholic clergy, the great majority of the Icelandic people did not welcome the Reformation. But it had been imposed by sheer force and everyone had to obey and bow to the will of the King, and his faith.

Great changes in religious and cultural life accompanied the Reformation, and many old practices were prohibited. All the cloisters were abolished and monks and nuns driven out. Catholic relics and works of art were forbidden, stolen or destroyed and the same happened with many old documents and manuscripts. People were forbidden to worship their old saints and everything that reminded of them was prohibited. All this was a great blow to Iceland's religious and spiritual life, in fact a cultural shock.

To make things even worse, the King removed a good deal of the revenues which had formerly accrued to the episcopal sees of Skálholt and Hólar. The first Lutheran bishops in the country were no great leaders either. They encountered huge problems in their work for the new Reformed Church, and could not cope with the King and his governors in directing the affairs of the Church and the schools, so they never had money enough to run them properly.

## Increased Royal Power

Once the King had brought about the Reformation by force, he and his governors and other officials took most of the power in Iceland into their own hands, and this greater and more direct foreign rule was felt more keenly than ever before. The lawmen and the old parliament lost much of their former power and influence, doing little more than approve and expedite the matters sent to them. Increasing legislative and judiciary power alike was now concentrated in the hands of the King and his officials, and the country was mostly governed from Copenhagen.

After the Reformation the King also became a great landowner in Iceland. He had seized all the lands owned by the monasteries, and as the supreme head of the Church he administered all its estates as well. Rents, taxes, fines, duties and revenues of all kinds now began to flow into the royal treasury on a far greater scale. Until the Reformation the Icelandic people in general had been fairly well off, but after it they seemed to slide from prosperity to poverty, in slow, steady succession. In fact, since 1262, Iceland had been a country of its own with certain rights under the King. After the Reformation it resembled more and more an exploited colony.

Part of this new system of government was a new code of law on adultery and related charges. Severe laws from 1564, the Grand Court, stipulated not only high fines, but also the death penalty for a wide number of offences. Executions became commonplace, especially during the summer parliamentary sessions. Women were often drowned, while men were hanged or beheaded. These stern laws remained in force till 1838, although they were rarely enforced in their last decades.

## The Commercial Monopoly

The growing power of the King was nowhere felt as sharply as in the Iceland trade. English and German merchants had largely taken over from the Norwegians in the fifteenth and sixteenth centuries. For a long time they had competed and even fought occasional battles for this profitable trade. The Danish King sided with the Germans and in the sixteenth century the English were at last ousted from Iceland. German merchants, mainly from Hamburg, kept the trade mostly for themselves, and the Danes were too

*Magical letter used in witchcraft.*

weak to succeed in their attempts to take it over. Nonetheless, the King maintained a constant interest in it too, keeping for himself the most profitable Icelandic merchandise such as falcons, sulphur and to some extent cod-liver oil.

The contemporary economic philosophy of the mercantile system was spreading. In accordance with its doctrines, the King wanted to strengthen the position of his subjects and country through new industries, colonies and trade. By the end of the sixteenth century the townsmen in Denmark had grown so strong and numerous that the King felt the time had come for Danish merchants to take over the Iceland trade from the Germans. He therefore leased the whole Iceland trade in 1602 to certain merchants in three towns in Denmark: Copenhagen, Elsinore and Malmö. This was the beginning of the notorious commercial monopoly which lasted in one form or other for nearly two centuries, until 1787.

These leaseholders were the only merchants who were allowed to trade in Iceland. They could determine prices largely at will, sell their goods at exorbitant rates and buy Icelandic products cheap – which was precisely what they did. Iceland was divided into trade districts, and everyone had to buy and sell in certain stores on pain of brutal punishment. Merchants could even import bad and rotten goods, as there were no other suppliers to go to. The Icelandic people were in effect enslaved by this commercial monopoly, to become its servants. They complained in petitions to the King, but to little avail. Secret trading with merchants from third countries, like the Netherlands, England and Germany, was severely punished. It has been said that of the many plagues which have afflicted the Icelanders in the course of the centuries, the Danish trade monopoly was probably the worst.

## Superstition and Witchcraft

The seventeenth century was the age of religious controversies and wars. Fanaticism and superstition of all kinds were part of daily life, along with intolerance

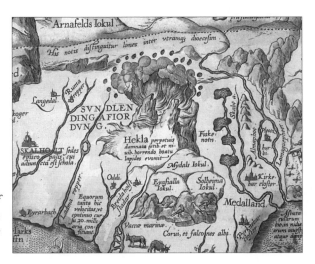

*From an old map of Iceland. The wolcano Hekla is shown in the middle.*

and terrible persecution of everybody who deviated in one way or other from the norm. Such were the consequences of the Reformation and Counter-Reformation on the European continent, where millions of people perished in wars, in the torture rooms of the Inquisition or at the stake. Even the Icelanders on their distant island had their share in the developments that were taking place in the outside world.

Superstition spread across Iceland like a gruesome epidemic, and learned men were even worse in this respect than the common people. If anything happened to a horse or a cow, it was instantly assumed to be due to the enmity and witchcraft of one's neighbours. The devil and his demons were seen to be at work everywhere, using man as their instruments. This led to accusations against and persecution of what can only have been innocent people. Burning at the stake was the acknowledged punishment for sorcery, costing no fewer than twenty-three people their lives in the years from 1625 to 1685. Of this number only one was a woman, contrary to the custom in other countries, where women were in the majority.

When the seventeenth century drew to a close, superstition ebbed slowly out with it and disappeared for the most part in the course of time.

Superstition was often connected with certain natural objects, for instance Mount Hekla, the most famous volcano in Iceland, which was widely believed to be the main entrance to Hell. After two Icelandic students from the University of Copenhagen climbed to the top if it in 1750 and returned safe and sound, popular fear of it began to wane. This was also the case with many other objects and phenomena once people began to learn more about them.

## Turks and Other Marauders

Despite his unparalleled power and revenues after the Reformation, the King almost entirely neglected to protect his faraway country, Iceland. Occasionally, pirates and other marauders of various nationalities would come to its shores to murder, rob and commit other atrocities. In 1579, English robbers committed a wave of crimes and held a rich nobleman ransom, and in 1615 Spanish whalers caused an uproar, but the Icelanders gathered forces and killed a number of them. In 1627 the country was attacked by pirates from Algeria. They stole and plundered all the valuables they could find, and killed a number of people. On leaving, they took several hundred men, women and children, mostly from the Westman Islands, as captives and sold them into slavery in North Africa. Relatives and others collected money to buy their freedom, but only a few – 37 out of 370 captives – succeeded in returning home many years later. These much-feared Algerian pirates were always called Turks in Iceland, because North Africa was then a part of the Ottoman or Turkish Empire.

## Absolute Monarchy in 1662

From ancient times, the King of Denmark had been elected by the estates. But, following the pattern in most European countries after the Reformation, the nobility lost power and the new class of townsmen grew stronger. When the nobility tried to obstruct the King, and neglected its duties towards the national defence, it was only natural for him to strengthen his position with the support of the burghers and the clergy.

This was what happened in Denmark after the war with Sweden, when the nobility had failed in the defence of the country and lost a good deal of land in what is now South Sweden.

In 1661 King Frederick III changed the government of Denmark and Norway so as to make himself and his heirs hereditary kings, by the grace of God, with absolute power to rule the realm free of all interference by the nobility or others. The following year, 1662, the Icelanders were supposed to swear an oath of allegiance to this absolute King. However, the Danish governor arrived too late for the summer parliamentary session at Thingvellir that year, so he summoned the lawmen, bishops and other delegates to an extraordinary session in Kópavogur, near Bessastadir.

The Icelandic leaders, lawspeaker Árni Oddsson and Brynjólfur Sveinsson, bishop of Skálholt, pleaded the case for preserving old national rights and protested against the new system of government. But the governor did not listen, simply pointing to his soldiers nearby and asking if they did not see them. The Icelanders had no choice but to give in, and eventually signed their names where they had been ordered to, reputedly with tears in their eyes.

*The colonial governor's residence at Bessastadir, old drawing.* With the introduction of absolute monarchy in 1662, the Old Treaty of 1262 and its later amendments were abolished. The King by the grace of God enjoyed exclusive power for the next two centuries.

# National Resistance

## *Printing and Publishing*

A new bishop, Gudbrandur Thorláksson, assumed office at Hólar in 1571 and ruled his diocese for fifty-six years, until his death in 1627. This uncommonly able and learned man did much to establish the Lutheran Church in the country in general. For instance, he instigated major reforms in the education of clergymen, improved their economic conditions as well, and did much to restore the Church and episcopal offices to their former glory.

But the bishop's most remarkable achievement was to start printing and publishing books at Hólar. Jón Arason, the last Catholic bishop, had brought a printing press from Hamburg about 1530 and set it up at a succession of places in Iceland. While the approaching Reformation and religious struggles of his time hampered him from extensive publishing work, it is known that he printed a liturgy and perhaps other similar literature. On acquiring this printing press, Gudbrandur Thorláksson brought it to Hólar, where he and his assistants then translated the Bible into Icelandic, and printed and published it in 1584. This was in fact the first book printed in Icelandic in the country, and proved to be of great importance for the religious and cultural life of the nation. Besides the Bible the bishop published a large number of other books, mostly religious, but also some other types of literature.

With his publishing work, Gudbrandur Thorláksson strengthened not only the cause of the new faith but, above all, of the Icelandic language, literature and general national culture. He can be thanked for the fact that Icelandic clergymen never delivered their sermons in Danish, as happened in Norway for instance. This remarkable bishop was very artistic too, carving all the ornate capital letters for his Bible with his own hand. Around 1600 he also drew up a new

*The Bible was first printed 1584 in Iceland.*

map of Iceland, which was much more detailed and accurate than earlier drafts.

Oddur Einarsson, who served as bishop at Skálholt from 1589 to 1630 and was a contemporary of Gudbrandur Thorláksson at Hólar, also did much to restore the religious and cultural life in his diocese and was himself a highly educated and literary man too. For instance, he wrote much himself and encouraged other learned men to write histories of the Reformation and other major recent and contemporary events. Such cultural activity was a new departure, because very little literary work such as history and saga writing had been undertaken in the two centuries from 1400 to 1600.

### Some Poets and Writers

In spite of economic decline, poverty and hardship in the sixteenth and, even more, in the seventeenth centuries, a large number of poets and other writers were active. Among them was the excellent poet Einar Sigurdsson (1538–1626), some of whose poems were published at Hólar. Then there was Hallgrímur Pétursson (1614–1674), one of the greatest poets in the history of Iceland, and best known for his Passion Psalms about the sufferings and crucifixion of Jesus Christ. His contemporary, Stefán Ólafsson (1619–1668), was another fine poet. Björn Jónsson (1574–1655) was known for his annals, histories and other works. Arngrímur Jónsson the Learned (1568–1648) was a great scholar. Outraged by the absurd ideas some foreign writers of his time had about Iceland, he wrote several books in Latin about the country and its history, which he published abroad. Another great scholar of this age was Gísli Magnússon the Wise (1621–1696), who had studied at several universities abroad. Back home he was a leader of a national restoration movement, not only in cultural affairs but also in commerce, mining and agriculture, on which he wrote learned essays. Brynjólfur Sveinsson (1605–1675), another accomplished scholar, served as bishop at Skálholt from 1639 until just before his death and

*Bishop Gudbrandur Thorláksson who printed and published The Bible in Hólar 1584*

was an avid promoter of both religious and cultural activity. Yet another bishop at Skálholt, Jón Thorkelsson Vídalín (1666–1720), was an excellent writer whose very popular book of Family Sermons remained in use for some two centuries. Thormódur Torfason (1636–1719) was a man of learning who worked as a historian in the service of the Danish King. Among his greatest works are histories of Norway and other Nordic countries.

## Precious Manuscripts

*Árni Magnússon historian and collector of old manuscripts.*

In the seventeenth century, the Danes and Swedes began to take a great interest in their nations' past. The absolute monarchs of this time wanted accounts of their ancestors and histories of their glorious deeds to strengthen their own position. Since Iceland was the only country where the medieval history of other Nordic countries had been written down and preserved, something of a scramble began between Denmark and Sweden to collect old manuscripts there. As the country belonged to the Danish King he acquired the most, although the Swedes also gained some very rare and precious manuscripts.

Árni Magnússon (1663–1730), an accomplished Icelandic scholar and professor of history at the University of Copenhagen, collected all the documents and manuscripts he could find in his own country and took them back with him to Copenhagen. These antiquities were later collected in a library at the university, which at this time was not only the university of Denmark, but of Norway, Iceland, the Faroe Islands and other tributary countries as well. In 1728 a terrible fire broke out in Copenhagen, destroying a large part of Árni Magnússon's library and dealing Iceland an irreparable loss. Most of the oldest manuscripts, however, were saved from the conflagration. Heartbroken by this tragedy, the scholar and patriot did not live long afterwards. He used to say to his friends: "My pleasure in life has gone and nobody can give it back to me."

# The Age of Enquiry

## The Registration Commission (1702–1712)

The closing decades of the seventeenth century were difficult in many ways. The climate was cold and was accompanied by growing and almost endemic poverty. Near the end of the century people died of starvation in their thousands and few courses of action seemed open for alleviating this adversity. In 1700, at the same time as they swore their oaths of allegiance to the newly crowned King Frederick IV, the Icelandic delegates asked the King to help relieve the sufferings of their people. The new King and his counsellors saw that something clearly had to be done to reverse this growing poverty and dearth in Iceland. It was to his advantage, in fact, since fewer revenues could be expected from a country whose people were so badly off. The outcome was a two-man commission which the King sent in 1702 to investigate the situation in Iceland and make proposals for improvements.

These two commissioners were learned Icelanders, scholar Árni Magnússon and his lawyer friend Páll Vídalín. Their first task was to conduct a general nationwide census in 1703, when the total population proved to number only 50,358 inhabitants. In the course of the next few years they inspected and registered properties all over the country and prepared a roster of all farms with a complete description of their belongings. But much of their time was spent clashing with unjust Danish merchants, whose conduct towards the local people they tried to improve. They also tried to improve the conditions of the numerous tenants and lighten the burdens imposed on them, as well as rectifying various wrongs committed by government officials and judges, and helping the victims of injustice, when it was not too late.

The commissioners spent ten years on their task and did a very useful job. But while this was under way a new blow struck Iceland: a terrible smallpox epidemic

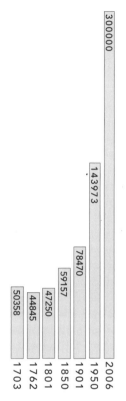

*Iceland's population dwindled in the 18th and 19th centuries, to its lowest level since the settlement, then it began to rise.*

in 1707, which killed about 18,000 people, or more than one third of the population.

## *Messengers of Pietism (1741-1745)*

In the eighteenth century a religious revival took place in many Protestant countries, known as Pietism. When it spread to the Danish clergy and even the royal court, the authorities felt it was necessary to help the Icelandic people in this respect as well. In 1741, two theologians, Icelander Jón Thorkelsson and a Dane, Ludvig Harboe, were sent on a mission to Iceland for this purpose. They travelled the country for years, visiting churches and clergymen. Among the many things they did was to enact rigid regulations on the upbringing of children and on education in general, and to preach against saga literature and traditional ballads as supposedly bad for the spiritual welfare of the people. Their visit resulted in some necessary reforms to the cathedral schools at Skálholt and Hólar, and more stringent demands on clergymen.

These two emissaries, particularly Ludvig Harboe who later became bishop of Zealand and remained favourably disposed towards Iceland for the rest of his life, stressed the necessity of reading religious books. All children were expected to be able to read before their confirmation about the age of fourteen. Confirmation had been introduced by law in the Danish kingdom in 1736 and was put into force in Iceland in 1744 with new regulations set by the visiting Pietists. On the whole, this tour of inspection had a beneficial and stimulating effect on Icelandic cultural life. Afterwards, Jón Thorkelsson went back to Denmark for the rest of his life. He bequeathed all his wealth as a legacy to Iceland for the purpose of educating poor children in the southwest part of the country, and the fund was used to run a school for many years.

## *Survey of Natural Resources (1752-1757)*

Interest in Iceland clearly began to grow in Denmark

*"Classical" timber and turf-roofed farmhouse of fairly wealthy gentry.*

at this time. In 1752, two young Icelandic students of natural science at the University of Copenhagen, Eggert Ólafsson (1726–1768) and Bjarni Pálsson (1719–1779), were sent on an expedition to investigate Iceland's natural resources and the culture and customs of the people. They spent several years travelling all over the country and conducted some excellent research. Eggert Ólafsson collected his findings in a lengthy report called the Book of Travels, which was translated into other languages and still remains today a remarkable source of information about Iceland in the eighteenth century.

Both these men returned to Iceland on finishing their studies. Bjarni Pálsson was appointed the first chief physician in Iceland when that office was established in 1760. Eggert Ólafsson was appointed governor, but died before taking office. Deeply patriotic, he was also an excellent poet, writing exhortations to the people to strengthen the national cause and work well for their country. Few if any Icelanders have been so deeply lamented by so many as Eggert, when he was lost at sea at a relatively young age.

## The Committee of 1770–1771

In 1770 the King dispatched another committee, comprised of an Icelander and two Danes, to investigate why so much had gone awry in Iceland and make proposals for improvements. They gathered plentiful information and pointed out a variety of useful possibilities. Among their ideas was that farmers should be encouraged to increase cultivation and production, and given financial support for doing so. Suggested activities included growing grain, potatoes and other vegetables, the use of handmills for grinding grain in their homes, the enclosure of fields and building of new farms. The committee also proposed a number of new industries, more fishing and better processing of fish products, bigger and better fishing vessels, and so on. Improvements were recommended in communications through road-making, the building of bridges and the establishment of a postal service. Very few of these ideas were realized at the time, although the mail service was introduced in 1776.

Investigations into conditions in Iceland continued throughout the eighteenth century. One such investigator was Ólafur Ólafsson, who called himself Olavius. He wrote a book of observations made on his travels through the country in 1775–77, suggesting such improvements as increased fishing and shipping, and the restoration and resettlement of deserted farms. Near the end of the century, physician and naturalist Sveinn Pálsson recorded various observations, including the first scientific theories to be put forward about the nature and movements of glaciers.

It must be admitted that the King and his counsellors made genuine efforts at this time to discover possible ways of helping Iceland. One innovation which was thought to be beneficial was to bring reindeer from northern Norway to Iceland, in 1771. Although the experiment was later repeated several times, Icelandic farmers never learned to herd these animals as livestock. Ever since this time, reindeer have lived wild in certain parts of the highlands.

# The Age of Development

## *An Icelandic Bailiff (1749)*

The Danish governors and other officials had their headquarters at Bessastadir, near Reykjavík. Some of these high officials only stayed for a short time and a few did not come to the country at all. Instead, they delegated their duties to bailiffs, who were often very rude and brutal officials. Bailiffs had always been of Danish nationality until 1749 when an Icelander, Skúli Magnússon (1711–1794), was appointed to the office. At first his appointment drew astonishment, for the general belief was that no Icelander could be evil enough to become a bailiff. But Skúli Magnússon proved to be different from his predecessors, and did an excellent job.

He had earlier served as district sheriff and was known as a capable and determined man. He had also written at length about economic affairs and tried to promote improvements in commerce and industries. In his new office as bailiff he often clashed with Danish merchants, attempting with some measure of success to make them trade fairly, charge reasonable prices and not import rotten and worm-eaten grain and goods, although they resisted him and tried to defame him abroad. But Skúli wanted to do more. Uncommonly progressive in outlook, he dreamt of free trade and general improvements in both the industrial and everyday life of his people.

## *New Industrial Workshops (1752)*

On becoming bailiff, Skúli Magnússon not only talked and wrote about progress and improvement. He set to work and interested several other prominent figures in his ideas. Even the King became interested and favoured his initiative. These ideas and plans were discussed in the 1751 parliament and a company with a number of stockholders was established. The King gave the farm of Reykjavík along with several others

*Reykjavík in the late 18th century.*

to the company and invested considerable sums in it too. In 1752 Skúli Magnússon started to build several workshops in Reykjavík for crafts including the spinning, weaving and dyeing of woollen goods, tanning of skins, spinning of fishing lines, and production of salt and sulphur. The company bought decked vessels for fishing and introduced better methods of curing fish for export. Improvements were also planned in agriculture, and farmers trained to grow grain and vegetables and cultivate trees. Potatoes had not yet reached Iceland at this time but were introduced a little later, in 1758 at Bessastadir and in 1759 in the west by an ingenious clergyman, Björn Halldórsson, who experimented widely and wrote a number of useful books on the subject. Farmers were urged to enclose their fields with fences, and a new breed of sheep was imported to improve the quality of the wool, although this move was to do more harm than good, because with them came the highly contagious disease of scab which would plague local stocks long afterwards. A great many new implements and machines were brought in as well, such as the spinning wheel to replace the old spindle, and a new kind of loom.

The company had its headquarters in Reykjavík,

where a number of houses and workshops were built. Some industries were also located in Hafnarfjördur and elsewhere. All went well for a while, but the company was always strapped for funds in spite of substantial support from both King and government. The directors of the company and its various operations also had to fight the ignorance of the working people, unfavourable natural conditions and the envy and enmity of the Danish merchants who felt this venture could only flourish at their expense. Amid mounting debts the company and workshops were taken over in 1764 by the Danish monopoly company which held the Iceland trade at that time. Skúli Magnússon was soon ousted from the board, and the workshops declined and gradually disappeared over the next few decades.

## The Beginning of Reykjavík

Skúli Magnússon's vision of new industries, a fishing fleet, agriculture, mining and free trade was not realized through this venture. But he had not worked in vain, for his ideas lived on and much had been learned, despite countless mistakes and failures, from his initiative and experiments. And the houses and workshops he had built in Reykjavík remained. Merchants, officials, craftsmen, fishermen and workers began to settle down in this little village.

This was the beginning of Reykjavík, the future capital of Iceland, on the estate of the first settler, Ingólfur Arnarson. If Ingólfur had laid the foundation for the settlement of Iceland with his farmhouses in Reykjavík in 874, it was Skúli who laid the foundation for the City of Reykjavík with his houses and workshops in 1752. This little village grew very slowly at first, and when Reykjavík was granted its municipal charter in 1786 it had a mere 167 inhabitants.

*Sheriff Skúli Magnússon, statue by Guðmundur Einarsson.*

## New Buildings of Stone

Houses in Iceland had not been built of any lasting material until the eighteenth century. Permanent buildings were part of the general process of develop-

91

*The oldest buildings in Reykjavík, dating from about the middle of 18th century: house and chapel on the island og Videy, built for Skúli Magnússon.*

ment, when several relatively large houses were constructed which are still in use today. The oldest was on Videy Island, built as his official residence by the indefatigable bailiff Skúli Magnússon in 1754. Then came the Nesstofa for the head physician and the Hólar Cathedral in 1763. A large house at Bessastadir for the governor and other high officials was finished in 1766. It was used as a school in the first half of the nineteenth century and is now the official residence of the President of Iceland. A new prison was finished and opened in the centre of Reykjavík in 1771, subsequently converted into a government building for the highest Danish and later Icelandic officials, which now houses the offices of the Prime Minister of the Republic. From this time also date the church on the Westman Islands and Reykjavík Cathedral which was completed in 1796 but later enlarged and changed to its present appearance.

# Hard Times

## The Laki Eruptions (1783–1784)

In the latter half of the eighteenth century numerous occurrences would harass and torment the Icelanders. Unfavourable natural conditions, volcanic eruptions and epidemics and diseases afflicting both people and animals nipped many efforts towards improvements and progress in the bud. The years 1752–1759 were a continuous spell of bad agricultural seasons, bringing starvation and the abandonment of many farms. Compounding these problems were terrible eruptions in the volcanoes Katla in 1755 and Hekla in 1766.

By far the worst of all these calamities, however, were the Laki eruptions which began in the spring of 1783 and lasted for about one year. Laki is a huge volcanic rift to the west of the vast glacier Vatnajökull in the southeast of Iceland. A gigantic quantity of glowing lava tumbled from these craters in the highlands and down to the lowlands where it spread and eventually covered an area of 565 km2, which is said to be the world's largest lava field created in historical times by a single eruption. Numerous farms were damaged or destroyed and people in the region fled in panic.

Accompanying the eruptions, toxic gas filled the air. It poisoned vegetation, eventually killing off the animals. An intense shortage of food followed, bringing terrible famine to most parts of the country. Hordes of starving beggars roamed the countryside, but had little chance of finding anyone with food to spare. It has been estimated that between nine and ten thousand people died of starvation in the years 1783–84, and the population fell below 40,000 again.

Great earthquakes also occurred around the same time, in 1784, wreaking damage and bringing down houses and other buildings, especially in the southern quarter of the country. In Skálholt, for instance, all the buildings except the church were flattened, and the bishop transferred his office and the school to Reykja-

*The great Laki craters west of the Vatnajökull glacier erupted in 1783 with devastating consequences.*

vík, although this move was not officially declared permanent until 1796.

The King and his government sent help from Copenhagen in the form of money and food, and although this proved helpful, in many instances the action came too late. A committee was appointed to work on the Iceland problem and there was even talk of evacuating the country and moving either some or all of the inhabitants to Denmark. But it never went so far. These terrible years passed by and the nation slowly began to recover.

A wealth of literature remains describing these hard times. The most famous source is perhaps the autobiography of the Reverend Jón Steingrímsson (1726–1791), who was serving as a clergyman in the districts where the lava flow came down. Local people believed that he had even stopped the glowing lava just outside the church of Kirkjubaejarklaustur in 1783, during a divine service as he delivered what would later be called the "Fire Sermon".

## The Trade Monopoly Repealed (1787)

Governmental authorities in Iceland and Copenhagen tried hard to alleviate conditions in Iceland after all the catastrophes in the latter half of the eighteenth century. The free trade advocated by bailiff Skúli

Magnússon had been met with hostility by the Danish merchants, who claimed it would only make a bad situation worse. But now Skúli's views met with more understanding in Copenhagen. Also working for the same cause was Jón Eiríksson (1728–87), a learned Icelander in the service of the King.

Through the influence of Skúli Magnússon, Jón Eiríksson and others, and in light of the suffering that was rife, it was decided at last to open up the Iceland trade in 1787, but only to subjects of the Danish King. This limited free trade had little impact in the beginning, but helped in the long run, even though it took the Icelanders a long time to take trade into their own hands.

### National Institutions Abolished

After the old episcopal see of Skálholt was destroyed for the most part in the great earthquake of 1784, the buildings were not restored and the bishop, Hannes Finnsson, moved away to settle in Reykjavík, where it was eventually decided in 1796 that the episcopal seat should remain in future. The school moved from Skálholt too and a new schoolhouse was built in Reykjavík in 1786. Hampered by being housed in this very poor building, it was moved again, to Bessastadir, in 1805, and remained there for several decades. The school later moved back to Reykjavík, to a new schoolhouse built in 1846 that is still in use. Towards the end of the eighteenth century the authorities also decided to abolish the episcopal see and school at Hólar. Influential men in the north opposed the measure fiercely, but in vain. The old institution of Hólar was abolished in 1801, leaving only one bishop and a single school in the whole of Iceland.

*Magnús Stepensen, an important figure at the beginning of the 19th century.*

Little remained, either, of the former glory of the old Althing parliament at Thingvellir. In 1798 it convened for the last time on the old parliament site, then moved to Reykjavík where it met over the next two years. In 1800 the King and prominent Icelanders agreed to abolish this old and, in their opinion, useless institution and establish in its place a superior national court to take its judiciary power. The first president of this new court was Magnús Stephensen, a member of a very powerful family. His father, Ólafur Stephensen, was governor of Iceland from 1790 to 1806, the only Icelander who ever served in that office. When the episcopal sees and schools at Skálholt and Hólar and the old Althing at Thingvellir had been abolished, there was, in fact, nothing from old times left to remind the Icelanders of their national identity and existence in their own country. Being deprived in this way of its ancient historical institutions must have been felt as a great blow to the pride and consciousness of a once-independent nation.

## Some Literary Men

The two last bishops of Skálholt, Finnur Jónsson (1704–1789) and his son, Hannes Finnsson (1739–1796), were both scholars who published some remarkable works. But by far the greatest poet of this time was Jón Thorláksson (1744–1819), who not only composed original verse but also translated such works as Milton's Paradise Lost into Icelandic. Sigurdur Pétursson (1754–1827 is also worthy of mention, as probably the first Icelandic playwright. Benedikt Jónsson Gröndal (1762–1825) was another fine poet, and Sveinn Pálsson (1762–1840) did some outstanding work in the natural sciences, as mentioned earlier.

# Unrest and Troubles

## Shipping Problems and Scarce Goods

The eighteenth century had treated the Icelanders
badly and nearly all attempts at improvements and
progress had come to nothing. Naturally the nation
took a long time to recover from this succession of disasters. Even the population had dropped from 50,358
in 1703 to 47,852 in 1801, owing to compounded
hardship and successive years of bad farming weather.
A Swedish scholar who travelled around Iceland late
in the eighteenth century wrote in his diary that very
seldom had he seen an Icelander smile.

In addition to all the troubles at home there were
troubled times on the seas in the late eighteenth and
early nineteenth centuries. Continual wars were being
waged between the great powers, Britain and France,
and their respective allies. First there was the American War of Independence, then the French Revolution,
and later the successive Napoleonic Wars until 1815
Warfare and blockades made all shipping difficult and
perilous, even for vessels from neutral countries. As a
consequence, shipping to and from Iceland was very
limited, causing a severe shortage of all necessities
which had to be imported, such as salt, iron, timber,
grain, fishing hooks and lines and countless other vital
items. Likewise, the same problems were faced in
sending Icelandic products to markets overseas.

The King of Denmark tried to preserve armed
neutrality in these wars, but after the battle of Trafalg-
ar and the continental blockade this position became
more and more difficult to maintain. Great Britain
feared Napoleon might gain control of the Danish-
Norwegian fleet and, when the Danish King kept on
sitting on the fence, struck first with an attack on Denmark in 1807, bombarding Copenhagen into surrender and towing the proud Danish-Norwegian fleet
away. After this violation Denmark became a close
ally of France and remained at war with Britain to the
bitter end in 1814. All shipping links with Iceland and

other Danish dependencies in the North Atlantic were jeopardized still further, caused great dearth in these countries.

## The Takeover of 1809

*Jörgen Jörgensen.*

In the hardship resulting from the Napoleonic Wars, the English were of great help in intermittently bringing goods to Iceland. In January 1809 an English freighter landed at Hafnarfjördur with many kinds of necessities, and after making an agreement with the Icelandic authorities, the English merchants sold their goods at reasonable prices. On board the ship was a Danish adventurer, Jörgen Jörgensen, who at the time was serving in the British navy and also working for a London soap-producer who wanted to buy tallow and cod-liver oil from Iceland for his factories.

In June the same year, Jörgensen returned, this time on a British frigate. When the English commissars, who had been left behind to take care of the trade, accused the authorities of trying to hinder it, Jörgensen and his British comrades promptly arrested the Danish governor, Count Trampe, and kept him in custody. On June 26, Jörgensen declared that all Danish authority and sovereignty over Iceland had been abolished for good. He issued a proclamation that he had personally assumed complete power as Protector of all Iceland and Chief Commander on land and sea. He promised the country British protection and said he would resign from office when a national convention had gathered and given the country a constitution the following year.

With this takeover of power Iceland had in fact become an independent state, which Jörgensen gave a new flag and a seal. He started to build a fortress near Reykjavík harbour and appointed eight young men as his bodyguard, whom he gave fine green uniforms. Most Icelanders remained indifferent to what was going on, and some of them thought that the English somehow stood behind this revolution. This was probably not the case, rather it was an act of adventure on Jörgensen's part, and although he may have enjo-

*"When the Lady Lost Her Wig": Jörgen Jörgensen, the Danish adventurer who seized power in Iceland in 1809, drew this picture during his imprisonment of himself dancing in Reykjavík.*

yed support by Englishmen privately, this was not given on a governmental basis. Most of the Icelandic and even some Danish officials sat on in office under Jörgensen's administration, but those who would not acknowledge the Protector were ordered to resign and new, more loyal men were appointed instead.

In the summer Jörgensen travelled to north Iceland to meet his subjects. Everywhere he tried to reorganize trade for the benefit of the Icelandic people, and seems to have been motivated by a general desire to help. Shortly after he returned from this long journey a British man-of-war arrived in Reykjavík. It was the Talbot, with Alexander Jones as commander. Jones had doubts about Jörgensen's behaviour in Iceland and knew he did not enjoy the support of the British government. The Danish governor did all he could to defame him and the rich and influential brothers, Magnús and Stefán Stephensen, also conspired against him. With their consent and support Commander Jones arrested Jörgensen and took him back to England.

In England Jörgensen went to prison but was soon released. A compulsive gambler, he was led by this habit into new troubles and transported to Australia. There he soon became a free man again and settled down in Hobart, Tasmania, where he died in 1841. He never returned to Iceland, the country where he had ruled as King for about two months in the summer of 1809.

After the Jörgensen episode, life in Iceland fell back into its old pattern again. But one thing had changed. Jörgensen had opened the eyes of the Icelanders to the fact that it was possible to live without the King in Copenhagen, and some of them slowly started to think about the possibility as a distant dream.

## The Union of Iceland and Norway dissolved

When France eventually lost the Napoleonic Wars, Denmark suffered badly because the victors agreed on punishing it for supporting Napoleon. In Sweden a French general, Jean-Baptiste Bernadotte, later King Karl Johan, had been appointed heir to the throne; although he had served under Napoleon, he later sided with his enemies. Sweden had lost Finland to Russia in 1809. In the settlement of 1814 this was made up for by taking Norway away from the Danish King and giving it to Sweden. Iceland had originally come under the King of Norway in 1262 and followed Norway under the Danish crown a little more than a century later. From that time on Iceland had always been counted with Norway in the realm of the Danish King. But in 1814 these two countries were disunited, and Iceland followed Denmark, along with the Faroe Islands and Greenland.

In 1814 the Norwegians revolted against the union with Sweden, led by a Danish prince, Christian Frederick, who had been governor of the country and would later rule Denmark as King Christian VIII. Under his leadership the Norwegians established their own free and independent kingdom and introduced a very liberal constitution. Sweden responded by invading, and after a short war Norway was forced into a personal union with the Swedish King but was allowed to keep its constitution for the most part. This union lasted for nearly a century, until 1905, when the Norwegians revolted again and it was dissolved peacefully. The Norwegians then established their own kingdom at last.

*King Christian VIII of Denmark.*

## Some Cultural Trends

*Rasmus Christian Rask, the Danish philologist who promoted the cause of Icelandic language and culture.*

During the early nineteenth century the Icelandic language was not held in great esteem, and probably enjoyed less respect than at any other time. Many officials and educated men used Danish more than Icelandic, and in the country's only school for higher education Icelandic was not even on the curriculum. But among the common people the language lived on in its pure and original form, maintained by the vigorous old saga tradition and flourishing poetic ballads. And of course there were poets at all times, major and minor.

Magnús Stephensen (1762–1832), president of the Superior Court in Reykjavík, was the period's leading cultural figure in many ways. An adherent of rationalistic philosophy, he published a large number of books and periodicals in that spirit. He also controlled the only printing press in the country, although he showed little concern for the Icelandic language. Another high official, Bjarni Thorarensen (1776–1841), was a lyrical poet of great stature, and while admiring classicism also ushered in Romantic ideas against dry rationalism. With his poetry he contributed much to the language and widely strengthened the national cause. For instance, one of his poems was adopted as a national anthem and sung to the tune of the British anthem for a long time. Yet another cultured high official of this time was Jón Espólín (1764–1836), whose chronicles are still of major importance for historical research.

A Danish scholar, the renowned linguist Rasmus Christian Rask (1787–1832), was one of the first foreigners to study and write about the Icelandic language. Among his many contributions to Iceland's cultural life was the establishment of the Icelandic Literary Society in 1816. Another Danish benefactor was Carl Christian Rafn (1795–1864), who founded a society to publish Old Icelandic literature. He was also a leading participant in the establishment of a library in Reykjavík in 1818, which would later become the National Library of Iceland.

# Dawn of Freedom

## New Political Currents

After the Napoleonic Wars a strong political reaction prevailed in most countries of Europe. But the reaction was countered by the July Revolution in France in 1830, when a very conservative King was replaced by a more liberal one. The waves from this revolution even reached Denmark and kindled some liberal movements there.

People in the duchies of Schleswig and Holstein, which to a great extent were inhabited by Germans, began to demand more political rights. The absolute King of Denmark refused to yield any of his power, but agreed to establishing General Estates or advisory assemblies in different parts of his state, where representatives of various classes could meet and pass resolutions and proposals for the King to approve or reject. These assemblies were envisaged, one for the duchies, one for Jutland and one for the Danish Islands.

The Icelanders were dissatisfied at not being granted an assembly of their own like other subjects of the King, but told to send two representatives to the Danish Islands' assembly instead. In their discussions for a better arrangement, progressive Icelanders began to raise the idea of restoring their ancient Althing.

## Student Idealism

At this time there were many Icelandic students at the Copenhagen University. Most were strongly influenced by the new Romantic thinking, and very nationalistic in their outlook. It did not satisfy their idealism in the slightest to send a few representatives from Iceland to discuss Icelandic affairs in a Danish advisory assembly. Instead, they dreamt of restoring the old Althing at Thingvellir. One of them was law student Baldvin Einarsson (1801–1833), who in 1829 launched a periodical where he put forward his ideas about a new national assembly in Iceland itself, and about a general awakening of industrial, cultural and national life. He was killed in an accident in 1833, only a year after graduating, but in his short life he accomplished much and lit a torch of freedom for those who came after him.

Two years after Baldvin Einarsson died, four young Icelandic students in Copenhagen started another periodical, Fjölnir, which was published on a somewhat irregular basis for nine years. While primarily a literary forum, the magazine also introduced new liberal ideas on cultural and political affairs. The so-called unwritten law of the Fjölnir group was as follows:

We will all be Icelanders,
We will protect our language and nationality,
We will have the Althing at Thingvellir.

*Romantic poet Jónas Hallgrímsson, a leading figure of the nationalist resurgence.*

These four young students were Jónas Hallgrímsson (1807–1845), a naturalist and outstanding poet in the Romantic vein, who made a major contribution towards reinvigorating the lyrical tradition and purifying the language; Konráð Gíslason (1810–1891), a linguist who would do much research in the interest of his mother tongue and become professor at Copenhagen University; Brynjólfur Pétursson (1809–1851), a law student who later worked in the government administration in Copenhagen; and Tómas Saemundsson (1807–1841), an idealist who wrote extensively about general progress, studied theology, and would serve as a clergyman in Iceland.

The Fjölnir group were sometimes felt to be on the radical side, and their ideas were by no means accepted by all their countrymen. But they had great influence, especially after their day, and cleared a way for national consciousness, progress and freedom later on.

## The Althing Restored (1843)

The Icelanders petitioned the King for their own advisory assembly instead of having to send their representatives to Denmark, and were even supported in these views by the Danish governor and high officials at the Danish court. The King responded by appointing a committee that was to meet in Reykjavík every other year to discuss schools and other Icelandic affairs. It met twice, but without great consequence.

When King Frederick VI died in 1839, his relative,

103

Christian VIII, came to the throne. The new King had been governor in Norway, and also ruled it as King during the revolt against Sweden in 1814, earning him a reputation as a fairly liberal and progressive statesman. Icelandic students in Copenhagen petitioned this new King for free trade and other reforms, but above all to be allowed to have their advisory assembly in their own country. The King agreed, suggesting to the Icelandic committee that it might be sensible to call this assembly by the old name "Althing" and hold it on the site of the old parliament at Thingvellir. This gesture was widely applauded and the King's message was greeted with delight by the students and Icelandic people in general.

Once it was decided to restore the Althing in accordance with the King's recommendations, a young Icelandic student appeared on the scene, clearly aware that it was his vocation to become leader of the new movement. This man was Jón Sigurdsson (1811–1879), a clergyman's son from the West Fjords, who would lead the Icelandic people from that moment until his death. From 1841 onwards he published a periodical, New Society, which was a forum for his ideas about political, economic, cultural and other affairs relating to the restoration of the Icelandic heritage and promotion of progress. He also put forward clear views about the restoration of the Althing. For him, the old arrangement was irretrievably lost, and this new assembly could never be the same as the old Althing, for which reason it should not be situated at Thingvellir, but rather in Reykjavík where the government and other high officials of the country were based. Reykjavík, he said, should become the centre of political and national life and serve as the capital of the new Iceland.

In spite of some opposition, Jón Sigurdsson's opinion prevailed. In 1843 the King decided to establish an advisory assembly for Iceland, the Althing, in Reykjavík. It met for the first time in 1845 with twenty popularly elected representatives and six members appointed by the King. Electoral rights were limited to property holders. The meetings were held in the new building of the Latin School in the centre of Reykjavík.

# Struggle for Independence

## *Farewell to Absolute Monarchy*

King Christian VIII was interested in political reforms and had plans to give both legislative and economic power to the people of Denmark. But he did not live long enough to realize these aims, dying at an early age in 1848. His son, Frederick VII, took over and was planning to go on with his father's reforms when a new revolution broke out in France in February 1848, which had widespread influence, even reaching Denmark. A revolt started in the Danish duchies of Schleswig and Holstein that led to three years of inconclusive war.

In Copenhagen, after popular demonstrations demanding democracy and political reforms in 1848, the King felt it was a wise move to renounce his absolute power and promise to meet these claims. The next step was to summon a national convention to give the Danish realm a constitution, and the King invited five representatives from Iceland to take part. But by this time the revolutionary waves had reached Iceland too, and with them the notion that any political reform should be decided in the country actually involved. The King then promised that no political changes concerning Icelandic affairs should be made until the Icelandic people had met in their own convention and presented their views and wishes. The Danish convention finished its work and on June 5, 1849 it consented to the constitution that replaced the absolute power of the King; ever since, this has been Denmark's national day.

Although Iceland did not see any real change in government at this time and the King, technically, still retained absolute power, a special office or department was set up in Copenhagen to handle Icelandic affairs, which was a sign of greater independence. In 1848 Jón Sigurdsson wrote an article in his paper outlining the main political strategies for his nation. He claimed on historical grounds that once the King had renounced absolute power, Iceland had thereby won back the same legal status it had earlier in conformity with the Old Treaty of 1262. Therefore the country was not part of Denmark at all, but only in a personal union through the King which both countries shared. At this point we can say the real struggle for Icelandic independence had begun.

## The National Convention (1851)

It took the King and government of Denmark a long time to make up their minds about the promised National Convention to determine Iceland's political future. The Icelanders made all necessary preparations, dividing the country into twenty constituencies with two representatives to be elected from each, making forty members in all, in addition to the six appointed by the King, as was the arrangement in parliament. The Convention was repeatedly postponed for reasons that included the war over the duchies in Denmark, until it was finally summoned in the summer of 1851. By then, however, the situation had changed, and the revolutionary waves from 1848 no longer rose so high in the outside world.

Endless discussions and meetings had taken place in Iceland in preparation for the Convention. On Jón Sigurdsson's initiative the main policy propositions agreed on by most Icelanders had been drawn up. Iceland demanded full political rights as a free country in a personal union with Denmark, with its own parliament with legislative and financial power and a home government to take care of all domestic affairs. Foreign trade was to be open to all and freedom of the press and other basic human rights were to be guaranteed.

The Danish government did not like such ideas at all, and when the Convention met at last in 1851 a contingent of soldiers was sent too, apparently to maintain law and order. The Icelanders did not understand such precautions because they had no intention of starting demonstrations and riots. When the King's deputy and governor of Iceland, Count Trampe (a relative of the Count Trampe who was in Iceland in

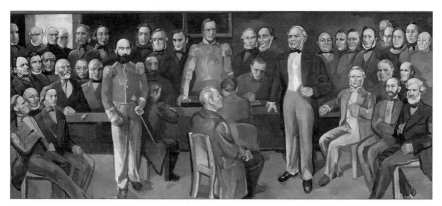

*"We all protest": Jón Sigurdsson confronting the Danish governor at the National Convention of 1851.*

1809), arrived to present the Danish proposals, it soon became clear that they would not bring much in the way of political reform. They would simply transfer Iceland's dependence from the King to the Danish parliament and effectively incorporate it into the Danish state.

While a committee of Danish and Icelandic representatives set to work to try and find a solution or compromise for this difficult situation, the King's representative announced the next meeting of the Convention for August 9. At the same time the Danish soldiers marched through the town and stationed themselves in the building next door to the Latin School where the meeting was being held. Probably the governor had seen that he would never get his proposals accepted, and in mid-debate he accused the delegates of time-wasting and dissolved the Convention without warning. Then Jón Sigurdsson rose and said: "In the name of the King and the nation I protest against this method and reserve for the Convention all rights to complain to our King against this lawlessness." Then virtually every representative rose and endorsed his words, saying: "We all protest."

But the Convention was dissolved and there was nothing left to do for the time being. The Icelanders met and sent resolutions to the King, but to no avail. It was clear that the Danish government would not do anything to meet the wishes of the Icelanders, and many officials who had opposed the Danish proposals were expelled from their posts. Thus ended the National Convention of 1851, leaving Iceland empty-handed. After this fruitless convention the Icelanders were sharply divided in their views of the Danes. On one side were Jón Sigurdsson and his progressive followers, and on the other many top government officials who supported the policy of the King and his government.

## A Constitutional Deadlock

After the failure of the 1851 Convention the Danish authorities tried several times to reach terms with the Icelanders about their constitutional ideas, but in vain. In 1861 a committee was established to make proposals about Iceland's financial and administrative affairs, which ruled that Denmark was heavily indebted to Iceland for all the land the King had taken from the monasteries and episcopal sees after the Reformation, and also because of the great wealth which had accrued to the Crown from the trade monopoly. It was proposed that Denmark should pay a yearly sum to Iceland in compensation, but since the committee could not agree on a figure the matter rested there.

In 1864 Denmark lost a war with Prussia and Austria over the duchies of Schleswig and Holstein, and had to surrender those territories. The Danes pressed hard to be allowed to keep part of Schleswig which had a largely Danish population, going so far as to offer Iceland in exchange for that region, but Bismarck refused to entertain such an idea. In 1863 a new King, Christian IX, had come to the throne of Denmark and would reign until 1906. He was said to be very conservative, but for Iceland he proved better than his reputation on many occasions. In 1865 a new governor for Iceland was appointed, Hilmar Finsen, who was a Dane but descended from a noble Icelandic family. Eager to find a political solution for Iceland, he drafted a bill in 1867 which would have granted the Icelanders both legislative and financial power. It was approved in the Althing, but rejected in the Danish parliament. The Danish government proposed a new bill in 1869 which did not go so far, and while this was approved in Denmark it was rejected in Iceland. After this the Danish government proposed its own constitutional law for Iceland and had it passed by parliament there.

*Governor Hilmar Finsen.*

## *The Enforced Constitutional Law (1871)*

The Danish parliament passed a constitutional law for Iceland in 1871 which stated unequivocally that Iceland was an inseparable part of Denmark, but with certain local rights. Under its terms, the Danish national treasury would pay an annual sum to Iceland and the Danish supreme court would be the highest court for Iceland, but in other matters Iceland would enjoy a certain amount of freedom. The Danish treasury contribution marked the beginning of Iceland's own national treasury. This law aroused great resentment in Iceland, especially for the fact that it was an imposed alternative to a rejected, more radical proposal. When the law reached the Althing a number of amendments were proposed, including that Iceland should have its own governor under the King instead of a Danish minister for Icelandic affairs in Copenhagen, and most preferably government by an earl in Iceland with his own ministry at his side. The King would not agree to these ideas, and the matter was shelved.

These constitutional points were discussed at a special meeting at Thingvellir in 1873. Many delegates were so enraged by the overbearing conduct of the Danish authorities that they said it would be preferable to emigrate than to suffer such injustice. The meeting accepted the original, rejected constitutional drafts again and they were passed by the Althing the same year. But the Althing passed a resolution urging the King, if he could not agree with the Icelanders, to present them with a constitution of his own devising the following year, 1874, when they would be celebrating the millennium of their country's settlement.

The Danish King and government paid little heed to the Icelandic opposition and the new law duly took effect. Among its provisions was to grant the governor a new title with the status of something like a viceroy. There were three men who served in this office from 1873 until Iceland first earned home rule in 1904: Hilmar Finsen, 1873–1884; Bergur Thorberg, 1884–1886; and Magnús Stephensen, 1886–1904.

### Free Trade (1854)

When nothing came of the 1851 Convention Jón Sigurdsson took up the battle for free trade. The notorious commercial monopoly had been abolished in 1787, but since the right to trade with Iceland was confined to subjects of the Danish King, it had always remained dominated by Danish merchants, even though a few Icelanders had penetrated their ranks. Danish merchants fiercely opposed extending commercial freedom, claiming it would only bring dearth and starvation to the Icelandic people. But the Icelanders were of a different opinion and passed many resolutions to that end. The King was frequently petitioned, often by people from different parts of the country. At last Jón Sigurdsson succeeded in winning support for his case from many liberal parliamentarians in Denmark and in 1854 the Iceland trade was made completely free and opened to everybody from April 1, 1855. Some benefits soon accrued, even

*From a 19th century store.*

though Danish merchants remained very influential for the next few decades.

## *Signs of Economic Growth*

In the nineteenth century farming still remained the main occupation in Iceland, followed by some fishing, as had been the case from times of old. Various improvements were made in housing and productivity was increased in the basic activities of farming and fishing in rural areas. In 1837 an agricultural society was founded in south Iceland which hired out consultants and made grants to stimulate progress among farmers. This farming union was extended to the whole country in 1899, giving rise to the Agricultural Society of Iceland.

For centuries foreign nations such as the English, French, Dutch and Spanish had been fishing in Iceland's rich waters, using much bigger and better ships than the local people who only had small, open rowboats for the most part. But in the latter half of the nineteenth century, Icelanders began acquiring larger, decked vessels, with modern fishing gear and sail-power instead of oars. This spelt a revolution in the fishing industry, and at the old coastal fishing stations new villages and towns began to grow up. A new urban class of fishermen and manual workers came into being.

*Sailing vessels of the 19th century.*

*Sveinbjörn Egilsson poet and linguist.*

*Poet Matthías Jochumsson, whose patriotic ode was adopted as the national anthem.*

Some Icelanders had become merchants when trade was liberalized after being in Danish hands for centuries. In 1869 a short-lived trading company was established in the northwest, followed in 1870 by a much longer-lasting enterprise in Akureyri under the direction of local entrepreneur Tryggvi Gunnarsson, which took over a large share of the trade in the north and east. Then, in 1882, the first cooperative trading company was established in Húsavík, also in the north, and cooperatives soon spread across the country. Iceland's trade was moving into local hands, albeit slowly.

The first savings bank was established in 1868, helping to channel funds into the growing industries. Book publishing became more common and more weekly newspapers began to appear after the first was launched in 1848.

## Schools, Poets and Culture

Education was not compulsory for children in the nineteenth century, although most of them learned at home to read and write. The task was entrusted to clergymen, since children had to be able to read the catechism and other religious books before their confirmation at the age of fourteen. Writing was not as necessary as reading, and even less so for girls than boys, according to the widespread nineteenth-century view. A few elementary schools were scattered throughout the country, the oldest established in Eyrarbakki in the south as early as 1852, and their number grew as the latter half of the century progressed. The only school for higher education was at Bessastadir from 1805 to 1846, when it moved to Reykjavík into a newly built schoolhouse which was also used for the meetings of the Althing for several decades. In 1847 a clerical seminary was established in Reykjavík, marking the first step towards academic education in the country.

In spite of poverty and adversity, cultural activity of some kind was also taking place. Some of the teachers at Bessastadir, for instance, were poets, or scientists.

*The Reykjavík Grammar School, built in 1846.*

There was Sveinbjörn Egilsson (1791–1852), a fine poet and linguist, who compiled a dictionary of the old scaldic poetic diction, the Lexicon Poeticum, and translated Homer's Iliad into Icelandic. Another teacher was Björn Gunnlaugsson (1788–1876), who travelled the country undertaking a geographical survey and produced a new, more accurate map. Also worthy of mention is Sigurdur Gudmundsson (1833–1874), who was not a teacher but a painter with an uncommon artistic awareness in his views and work, who started a collection of antiquities in 1863 that laid the foundation for the National Museum of Iceland. Magnús Grímsson (1825–1860) and Jón Árnason (1819–1887) collected and published a remarkable wealth of Icelandic folklore, adventures and legends, while Jón Thoroddsen (1818–1868) wrote and published the first real novel of the modern age.

Then a number of lyrical poets emerged in the latter half of the nineteenth century. The most famous was perhaps Matthías Jochumsson (1835–1920), whose works included the words to the Icelandic national anthem which was set to music by composer Sveinbjörn Sveinbjörnsson (1847–1927) and first heard at the millennial festival of 1874. Among the multitude of poets from this age are Steingrímur Thorsteinsson (1831–1913), Grímur Thomsen (1820–1896), Benedikt Gröndal (1826–1907), Kristján Jónsson (1842–1869), Hjálmar Jónsson (1796–1875) and Gísli Brynjólfsson (1827–1888). As the nineteenth century progressed, poetry became an increasingly vital factor in expressing and exalting the nation's struggle for freedom and independence.

113

# The New Era, 1874

*Sigurdur Gudmundsson painter and cultural figure.*

## The Millennial Celebration

In 1874 the Icelanders celebrated the millennium of the settlement of their country, since it was in 874 that the first settler, Ingólfur Arnarson, is considered to have taken up permanent abode in Reykjavík. Intense celebrations were held in Reykjavík and in most districts through the summer, but the most magnificent were at the national festival at Thingvellir in the beginning of August. On this festive occasion King Christian IX visited Iceland as the first sovereign ever to set foot on Icelandic soil. Moreover, the King brought with him the constitution for Iceland as had been agreed earlier.

These celebrations presented an unrivalled opportunity to display national identity and unity, and an opportunity for heartfelt rejoicing. They were attended by official delegates, newspaper reporters and private individuals from abroad, marked with fine gifts, and served to make Iceland better known to the outside world than ever before. Preparations and direction of the national festival at Thingvellir were in the hands of two men of the arts, photographer Sigfús Eymundsson and painter Sigurdur Gudmundsson.

The Danish royal visit aroused great interest for its novelty. The King stayed in Reykjavík, attended the festival at Thingvellir, then travelled quite widely and visited famous spots such as Gullfoss (Golden Falls) and Geysir, meeting the people on many occasions and receiving a heartfelt welcome everywhere.

## The Constitution of 1874

In January 1874 the King had announced he would bring Iceland a constitution when he visited it for the millennial festival, and so he did. This constitution was an addition to the Danish constitutional law for Iceland of 1871 and dealt mostly with domestic affairs. It decreed that legislative and financial power

*King Christian IX of Denmark arriving in Iceland for the millennial celebrational of 1874 to mark the thousandth anniversary of the settlement.*

was in the hands of the Icelandic parliament, the Althing, but that all laws had to be signed by the King before taking effect. Judiciary power was vested in courts, of which the supreme court in Copenhagen was the highest. Executive power rested with the King, but the minister for Iceland in the Danish government and the royal governor of Iceland in Reykjavík would largely handle Iceland's affairs in his name. There were also many provisions about basic human rights, such as freedom of speech and worship, the right to free trade and a free press, and so on. It was made a public duty to take part in the defence of the country, and no one unable to speak and write the Icelandic language would be eligible for public office. Parliament would assemble every other year and comprise thirty-six members, of whom thirty were to be chosen in a general election and six appointed by the King. Only males aged twenty-five or above and meeting a basic property ownership qualification had the right to vote.

The constitution was generally welcomed. While not meeting all the wishes and demands of the Icelanders, it represented an important step towards more freedom and independence. With its legislative and financial power in domestic affairs the Althing would be enabled to function much more independently and give better support to the industries, culture and general progress for the common good.

In addition, a new municipal law enacted in 1872 had taken effect in 1873, whose legislation on parish councils helped the many small communities to dispatch their duties and responsibilities more effectively. All this served to heighten the Icelanders' general self-awareness and train them in handling and governing their own affairs.

## A Nation Awakens

With the constitution secured, the Icelanders rose to the challenge of greater independence and set to work addressing countless general matters, for their country was poor and backward in most respects. But the people were optimistic and full of hope for the future.

In 1875 the currency was changed and the Króna introduced as the basic unit. Ten years later, in 1885, the first bank was established, the National Bank of Iceland, which helped emerging industries and businesses substantially. A new lucrative market for sheep emerged in England in the last quarter of the century, giving many farmers their first sight ever of gold coins. Butter would do likewise for others after the first dairy farms appeared at the dawn of the twentieth century.

*Goods and belongings ferried across a river.*

*Industrialist Otto Wathne, a leading figure in the developement of the fishing industry towards the end of the 19th century.*

Fishing was still for the most part conducted in the traditional fashion from open rowboats, but the number of decked vessels increased sharply after about 1870 and more effective fishing gear came into use. Motorized boats were first introduced in 1902. Cod was always the most important species of fish and was mostly cured in salt for export. Norwegians started a herring fishery off the east coast as early as 1868, and off the north coast shortly afterwards. The Icelanders soon learned from them the skills for catching and curing herring, which would create a very important industry in the course of time. The Norwegians also undertook intensive whaling and operated whaling stations in the fjords to the east and west, until the hunt was prohibited in 1915 because of dwindling stocks. Shark fishing was profitable for some time when the oil fetched good prices, but that was short-lived.

Communications in Iceland had always been difficult and hardly anything was done in the way of improvement until the last quarter of the century, when road-making and bridge-building began on a limited scale. The first large bridge was completed on the river Ölfusá in 1891 and another across the river Thjórsá in 1895, the most powerful and difficult rivers in the country, and more would soon follow. Communication by sea had always been easier than on land and in this period more consideration was given to the safety of seafarers. The first lighthouse was built on the Reykjanes peninsula in 1878 and more followed on various coastal sites.

At this time only a few elementary schools were to be found, but their number was to increase. A medical school was established in Reykjavík in 1876 as the second step towards academic education. Widespread reforms were introduced in farming in this period and four agricultural schools were established from 1880 to 1889. In 1874 a girls' school was founded in Reykjavík and in the following years schools of domestic science were set up in a number of rural places. In 1880 a secondary high school was established at Möðruvellir in the north and some twenty years later moved to Akureyri. A similar high school opened in Hafnarfjördur in the south in 1882. In recognition of the fact that education and training of seamen are necessary for a seafaring nation, a navigation college was founded in Reykjavík in 1891 after a number of trial schemes.

Health service was minimal in the nineteenth century and doctors rare, although this situation improved somewhat after the medical school opened in 1876. The first hospital was established in Reykjavík in 1866, and likewise a leper hospital in 1898 on the initiative of Danish Odd Fellows, a vital contribution towards countering an epidemic that had caused widespread suffering. And in 1902 the Catholic mission in Iceland opened the first modern hospital in Reykjavík.

Housing was mostly traditional with turf buildings predominating in the countryside, but timber became increasingly common in towns and villages. Late in the century concrete began to be used for houses and some fine buildings of stone were erected in Reykjavík, like the Prison and the House of the Althing in the centre of the capital.

The population grew quite sharply in the nineteenth century. In 1801 Iceland had only about 47,000 inhabitants, but by 1900 the number had risen to about 79,000, in spite of heavy emigration in the last decades of the century. At the same time people were beginning to move from the countryside into towns and villages. In 1801, for instance, Reykjavík had about 300 inhabitants, but by 1901 its population was 5,802.

## Jón Sigurdsson – The Pride of Iceland

The constitution of 1874 and many more political and other reforms in Iceland in the nineteenth century were the work, more than anyone else, of Jón Sigurdsson. He was the unfailing leader in his nation's struggle for freedom and independence from about 1840 until his death in 1879.

Jón Sigurdsson was born on June 17, 1811, at Hrafnseyri in the West Fjords where his father served as a clergyman. He did not attend school, being taught instead by his father at home. Later Jón studied lang-

*Jón Sigurdsson and his wife Ingibjörg Einarsdóttir. He was the leader of the nationalist movement and later inspiration of the process towards independence.*

uages, history and literature at the University of Copenhagen, and worked for a long time as a librarian and editor in Copenhagen. In 1841 he started to publish his own periodical, New Society, where he propounded his ideas about Iceland's national and political rights, free trade, schools and education, a health service and other reforms and general progress for the common good. He served as a member of the new parliament or Althing from 1845, and was for years the president of that assembly. Besides his writings in his own and other periodicals, he published a number of books. He and his wife Ingibjörg Einarsdóttir had no children of their own, but it was said that all Icelanders were like their children.

Jón Sigurdsson died in 1879. At his funeral in Reykjavík there was an inscription on a silver plate which read: "Jón Sigurdsson – the Pride of Iceland, its Sword and Shield." This inscription described the feelings of the people towards Jón Sigurdsson at that time, and still does. He has become a national hero and stands as a perpetual symbol of freedom.

## Emigration to America

Shortly after the middle of the nineteenth century a wave of emigration began from Iceland, mostly to North America. From 1856 onwards there was some emigration to Utah by Mormon converts. Shortly after 1860, a group moved to Brazil but emigration to that country proved short-lived. After 1870, however, for years in succession, large numbers of Icelanders uprooted themselves, boarded steamers and emigrated to North America. Some of them settled in Wisconsin and the Dakotas, but the great majority moved to Canada, where many were allocated land by the Canadian government and settled in large numbers on the plains and hills west of Lake Winnipeg in Manitoba. They made a treaty with the government in which they were guaranteed full citizenship rights but were allowed to keep their language and nationality, for themselves and their descendants. They called this settlement New Iceland. Initially they suffered great hardship, but soon adapted to their new life in the New World.

From 1870 to 1914 between ten and twenty thousand people left Iceland for North America. There were many reasons for this emigration. The farming weather was bad for years in succession, and in addition to the cold there was a terrible volcanic eruption in the Dyngjufjöll mountains in 1875 and a wave of devastating earthquakes in 1896. Then there was the prolonged political struggle with the Danish authorities which often seemed to produce little in the way of results. By this time travel had also become easier than ever and the governments of Canada and the United States actively encouraged immigrants from Europe, through agents working everywhere.

This emigration was a great loss for the Icelandic nation; although many emigrants left grudgingly, they had few opportunities to make a living in the old country and were simply seeking a better future for themselves and their descendants. Many prospered, too, in their new homes, and integration has never seemed a problem for them. Nonetheless, they have remained faithful to their language and heritage, hold-

*Tough living condition in Iceland led to widespred emigration to America.*

ing poetry and literature in as great esteem as their kinsmen "back home". More than a century later there is still an Icelandic newspaper in Winnipeg, Manitoba. The "Western Icelanders" have always had their own poets and writers, of whom the best known was perhaps Stephan G. Stephansson, or the poet of the Rocky Mountains, as he was called.

At the outbreak of the First World War this emigration stopped for the most part, but descendants of Icelandic emigrants have now spread all over North America.

## New Currents in Literature

As always, poets and writers exerted a major influence on Icelandic life in the last decades of the nineteenth and the first years of the twentieth centuries. In this period, Romantic poetry was giving way to a new movement, the realism strongly preached by certain literary talents in a new magazine, Verdandi, in 1882. The best-known prophets of realism were Gestur Páls-

*A living room in old times.*

*Poet Thorsteinn Erlingsson.*

son (1852–1891); Einar H. Kvaran (1859–1938), and the future political leader, poet Hannes Hafstein (1861–1922). Other writers of the period included the novelists Thorgils Gjallandi (= Jón Stefánsson, 1851–1915); Torfhildur Holm (1845–1918); Gudmundur Fridjónsson (1869–1944); Jón Trausti (=Gudmundur Magnússon, 1873–1918); and the poets Thorsteinn Erlingsson (1858–1914) and Einar Benediktsson (1864–1940). All these poets and writers and a number of others brought new elements into Icelandic literature and opened up new horizons in the national soul.

## The Struggle for Home Rule

The period from 1874 to 1904 witnessed fervent political debate over what system of government should be provided for in Iceland. After the death of Jón Sigurdsson in 1879 there were several standard-bearers, such as Benedikt Sveinsson, Jón Sigurdsson from Gautlönd, newspaper editors Björn Jónsson and Jón Ólafsson, and a number of others. They all agreed that the Icelanders themselves should wield much more executive power, and maintained that the best course would be for Iceland to have a governor or earl, based at home, to control all their country's domestic affairs. These ideas were very clearly set forth in resolutions made at a meeting at Thingvellir in 1885, and the Althing was largely of the same opinion. In 1889 a group in parliament under the leadership of Páll Briem tried to find a compromise between Icelandic and Danish points of view, but its ideas were rejected. The Althing stuck to former resolutions about home rule for Iceland, which the Danes rejected at once. It must be taken into account that the Danish government at the time was very conservative and would not tolerate any progressive ideas about political reforms in Iceland.

*Poet Einar Benediktsson.*

A new member of parliament was elected in 1894, Valtýr Gudmundsson, a highly gifted man and a professor at Copenhagen University. He very soon established himself as leader of a new parliamentary movement whose aim was to solve the political dispute between Iceland and Denmark. Its ideas were laid down in a bill put to parliament whose main theme was that an Icelander should take over the office of minister for Iceland, be responsible to the Icelandic parliament, but sit in Copenhagen. Although this bill was narrowly rejected in 1897, the movement caused a new political division in Iceland, between the faction of Valtýr Gudmundsson and the home rule party. Valtýr Gudmundsson's bill was rejected again in 1899, but then in a tied vote. By the 1901 parliament the Valtýr group had won a majority and the bill, somewhat refined, was passed in the Althing.

*Politician and scholar Valtýr Gudmundsson.*

Just as Valtýr Gudmundsson's cause finally triumphed in 1901, news came from Copenhagen of a hefty liberal victory and the formation of a new liberal government in Denmark. The leaders of the home rule party then wanted to try to secure more reforms for Iceland than had already been demanded. Alberti, the minister of Icelandic affairs in the Danish government, then summoned both Valtýr Gudmundsson and Hannes Hafstein, one of the leaders of the home rule party, to Copenhagen in the summer of 1901.

In Denmark, Valtýr Gudmundsson outlined his bill

about government for Iceland which the Althing had passed, and Hannes Hafstein set forth his party's views on home rule. The Danish government subsequently announced that it would put two bills to the 1902 Althing, one advocated by Valtýr Gudmundsson and the other based on the ideas of Hannes Hafstein and the home rule party. In the next general election in 1902 the home rule party won on the issue of a home minister, and confirmed a constitutional amendment to this effect in a new general election in 1903. The Danish authorities agreed and the King appointed Hannes Hafstein minister for Iceland, to take over the leadership from the royal governor on February 1, 1904. Iceland had won its long-desired home rule at last.

About the same time the Danish government agreed to a new coat of arms for Iceland with a falcon to replace the split cod which had been used for centuries. Ideas about a special national flag for Iceland were raised too. Most popular was the suggestion by poet Einar Benediktsson for a white cross on a blue background, but the issue lay dormant for the time being.

# Home Rule, 1904–1918

*Hannes Hafstein – The First Icelandic Minister*

It was a major event in the long struggle of the Icelandic people towards independence when the executive power of the government was moved from Copenhagen to Reykjavík and the Icelandic minister, Hannes Hafstein, took over from the royal governor on February 1, 1904. Hannes Hafstein was well known as a lawyer and politician and had held several offices before being appointed minister of Iceland, but was at the same time an idealist and man of enterprise, and eager to be of service to his country. He was also a man of great character, stately in appearance, famous as a poet and held in wide esteem.

*Hannes Hafstein, who became the first Icelandic minister under the home rule government of 1904.*

The legal status of Iceland altered little with this change in the constitution in 1904, because the Danish constitutional laws of 1871 were still in force and Iceland remained an inseparable part of the Danish realm. Its statutes about legislative and judiciary power were also still valid, but the base of executive power had changed and been transferred to Iceland itself. Governors and bailiffs disappeared, replaced by the minister and his cabinet in Reykjavík, which comprised three departments: ecclesiastical affairs and justice; industries and communication; and public finance. The minister was the head of them all and at his side stood the secretary of state as his deputy in the daily business of government.

*Development of Communications and Industries*

When the Icelanders had been given their own government at home, the new minister set to work in various fields. Firstly he went on with improvements to all kinds of communication within the country and with the outside world as well. A few bridges had already been built and more followed; road-building took a significant step forward. Wagons and carts came into use, although in many places packhorses had to con-

*The only railway ever built in Iceland, used for harbour construction work in the early 20th century.*

tinue to be employed for a long time to come. The first automobile came to Reykjavík in 1904 but proved of little use with so few roads in the country. Cars and lorries were not generally introduced until about a decade later. A wealth of new production equipment was brought in, such as separators, which along with the mechanized churn laid the foundation for butter production at the dawn of the century, and sewing and knitting machines. Several hydroelectric power plants were built after the first was set up in Hafnarfjördur in 1904. A gasworks was established in Reykjavík in 1910, while the first hydroelectric power station started up in the capital in 1921.

The fishing industry became increasingly important to the national economy. Open rowboats and decked vessels with sails were universal at the beginning of the twentieth century, but after the first motorized boat came to Ísafjördur in 1902, their use spread quickly to other fishing centres. Trawlers arrived shortly after that, effectively marking the beginning of fishing as big business. The first large trawler company was established in 1906 and more were soon to follow. A new bank, the Bank of Iceland, was founded in Reykjavík in 1904, largely with foreign capital, and lent money to these new fishing enterprises. Such investments, along with some Norwegian capital in the herring industry, laid the foundation for the mechanization of Icelandic fisheries.

In the first decades of the century the idea was raised of building railways in Iceland. A small rail track was laid in Reykjavík and used for a while to transport materials when the harbour was being built between 1913 and 1915, but was discontinued. Prohibitive costs, along with the fact that development of new roads and use of lorries began to escalate around that time, were the reasons why railways failed to establish themselves.

Certain enterprising Icelanders had bought and operated a few small steamships in the nineteenth century, but most shipping had still remained in the hands of Danish lines. In 1914, however, the Iceland Steamship Company was established with a massively subscribed public share issue drawing investors not only from all over the country but even from among Icelandic settlers in America, and Icelandic control of sea freight increased as a result. The town of Reykjavík grew rapidly early in the century, and although houses were still mostly built of timber, concrete began to be used to a far greater extent.

## The Arrival of the Telegraph

One of Hannes Hafstein's greatest achievements was to bring Iceland into contact with the outside world, through the telegraph. The need to establish a link had been frequently stated and some preparations had been made in this direction, but the minister himself brought the plan to materialization in 1905, when he

*Gullfoss, the first ship of the Iceland Steamship Company.*

signed a contract with the Great Nordic Telegraph Company regarding a cable installation from Scotland via the Faroe Islands to Seydisfjördur on the east coast of Iceland. Amid heated debate in the Althing, opponents of the plan claimed it was much more expensive an option than the wireless radio telegraph, recently invented by Marconi. Arguments about the plan escalated into demonstrations and riots, culminating in a mass lobby when some 300 farmers from south and west Iceland rode on horseback to Reykjavík to protest against the telegraph and try to persuade the minister to halt it. Hannes Hafstein tried to calm the demonstrators, but refused to entertain their demands, and his strong parliamentary majority duly ratified the treaty with the Telegraph Company. The cable was laid and the telegraph line from Seydisfjördur via Akureyri to Reykjavík was completed by autumn of the following year, 1906.

Over the next few years telegraph poles and wires were put up all around the country, bringing untold benefit for private and business communications both domestically and with the outside world. The telegraph and later the telephone soon won universal approval and the protests were forgotten. To give an indication of the importance of telegraphy, it has been said that only with its introduction did the Middle Ages finally come to an end in Iceland.

## *Schools and Academic Education*

In the first years of home rule much beneficial legislation was passed by parliament, and in the field of culture and education in particular a huge amount of work needed to be done. The first public education act was proclaimed in 1907, whereby all children were obliged to attend school from the age of ten to fourteen. In the course of time, compulsory schooling has been extended in phases, first applying from seven to fourteen, then from seven to fifteen, and by 1990 from six to sixteen years of age. Around the turn of the century there were few permanent schools, but their number gradually increased, first in towns and villages and then in the countryside. Despite intense building of schools, many places were only served by travelling teachers for a long time. In 1908 a teacher training college was established in Reykjavík, contributing greatly to the standard of general education.

Growing industrial mechanization called for more technical skills. The first technical training college opened in Reykjavík in 1904 and more would soon follow in other parts of the country. In 1905 a commercial college was set up in Reykjavík to meet the demand for trained business and clerical personnel.

Academic education, already represented by the clerical seminary from 1847 and a medical school from 1876, was boosted further when a law school was founded in Reykjavík in 1909. These three institutions were combined and, with the addition of a new faculty of philosophy, the University of Iceland was established in Reykjavík on the centenary of Jón Sigurdsson's birth, June 17, 1911. With the establishment of the university, far more students were able to receive a complete academic education in Iceland, instead of going abroad to complete their studies, as had once been customary.

Among other noteworthy legislation from this time was a law on land reclamation and afforestation in 1907, marking the start of the massive task of protection and restoration of vegetation which has been going on all over the country ever since.

## *Research and Science*

Scientific work and research in many fields increased in the first decades of the twentieth century. Among the contributions that were made, Thorvaldur Thoroddsen (1855–1921) investigated and wrote about Iceland's natural history; Stefán Stefánsson 1863–1921) studied vegetation and compiled a work on Iceland's flora; Bjarni Saemundsson (1867–1940) was a pioneer in fish and marine biology; Valtýr Gudmundsson (1860–1928) studied and wrote about ancient cultures; Jónas Jónasson (1856–1918) was a pioneer writer on ethnology, and Finnur Jónsson (1858–1934) and Björn M. Olsen (1850–1919) undertook research into the Icelandic language and literature. These scientists and many others laid the foundation on which much of Iceland's native research in various disciplines would later be based.

## Health and Sanitary Improvements

The health service was another sphere in need of massive development at the turn of the century. Doctors were stationed in different districts all over the country and hospitals were built in the main towns. Serious infectious diseases like leprosy and hydatids were eradicated for the most part, a psychiatric hospital was established in Reykjavík in 1907, and a campaign against tuberculosis began, with the completion of a sanatorium at Vífilsstadir just outside the capital in 1910 and another at Kristsnes in the north in 1927. The fight against TB was long and hard, and victory did not come until after the middle of the century, when it was to all intents and purposes eradicated.

Better sanitation also helped to improve general health. Water systems and drainage became widespread once the first water conduit and sewer pipes had been introduced in Reykjavík in 1909. As the economy prospered, people could afford better quality food and a more varied diet, which in turn contributed to raising national health standards.

## Temperance Movement and Prohibition

Alcoholism had long been a serious problem. Temperance movements had worked sporadically with scant success until 1884, when the International Order of Good Templars took root in Iceland, with the first IOGT lodge set up by Fridbjörn Steinsson in Akureyri in 1884. The movement spread nationally and a number of lodges were founded, greatly reducing public alcoholism. Teetotallers led a long campaign for complete prohibition of alcoholic beverages. Leading cultural and political figures joined forces with the movement and parliament passed a prohibition act in 1909, a year after a national referendum in favour of the move. Prohibition took full effect in 1915 and public drunkenness disappeared for the most part, in spite of some home brewing and smuggling.

But the prohibition did not last for long. It was partially repealed in 1922 when the import and sale of Spanish wines were allowed again, as a reciprocal measure to support the market for saltfish in Spain. An intense campaign ensued to abolish prohibition, which was finally repealed in 1934 after another referendum. Strong beer, however, remained prohibited right up until 1989. Since 1934, the Icelandic state has held a monopoly on all alcohol sales, which makes a substantial contribution to treasury finances.

## *Beginning of the Labour Movement*

For centuries, Iceland had been almost entirely a rural society based on cattle and sheep farming, which meant that the ideology of socialism made a relatively late appearance and had few adherents at first. Towards the end of the nineteenth century poets like Gestur Pálsson and Thorsteinn Erlingsson preached socialist ideas to some effect. With rapid growth in the fishing industry, wool mills and various kinds of workshops, and the beginning of towns and villages, a working class emerged. The first labour unions were founded in 1894, but were too weak to make significant claims on the employers at first. But the idea lived on. Printers established a union in 1897 and at last, after a strong broad union was finally launched in Reykjavík in 1906, the labour movement began to take shape.

Class antagonism became more distinct during World War I and in 1915 the first socialist party was founded in Akureyri by Ólafur Fridriksson, who then moved to Reykjavík. There he helped lead the first successful strike made by trawlermen, in 1916, and the improvement they won in their conditions showed clearly the new movement's immediate strength. Diverse and dispersed labour unions from all over the

*Ólafur Fridriksson, leader of the socialist movement.*

*Jónas Jónsson, one of the most influential politicians of his day.*

*Bríet Bjarnhéðinsdóttir, campaigner for women's rights.*

*Ingibjörg H. Bjarnason, who in 1922 became the first woman to be elected to parliament.*

country met and founded their national federation in 1916. The labour movement was then closely connected with socialist currents and in 1916 the Social Democratic Party was founded as one of its wings. Jón Baldvinsson, the SDP's first leader, also very soon became the chairman of the Federation of Labour Unions.

One influential political figure of the time was Jónas Jónsson, who had helped to establish both the Social Democratic Party and the Federation of Labour Unions. Nonetheless, he felt that workers and farmers should be in separate political parties and work together and support each other when it was suitable and mutually beneficial. With this ideological background the Progressive Party, which was mostly supported by farmers, was founded in 1916, with Ólafur Briem as its leader. Political debate intensified over this period, partly due to the appearance of daily newspapers. The first daily began in 1910 and another followed in 1913, both of them tending towards conservatism, while a Progressive Party daily was launched in 1917 and another supporting the Social Democrats in 1919.

## Women's Rights

Women had traditionally been excluded from public life and did not enjoy full political equality with men. Near the end of the nineteenth century they began their campaign for equal rights, championed by Bríet Bjarnhédinsdóttir (1856–1940) who was involved in almost all the progress and reforms that women won in her lifetime. The Icelandic Women's Society was established in 1894 and the Federation for Women's Rights in 1907.

Slow but gradual successes were scored by the equal rights movement. Women were granted franchise and eligibility as candidates for municipal elections in 1908 and the same year four women were elected to Reykjavík town council. In 1911 they were officially acknowledged as having equal rights to men for higher education and public office. Eventually, in 1915, women aged forty and over were given the right to vote and stand in parliamentary elections, and the age limit was subsequently reduced to that of males in 1918. The King signed the amendment to the constitution granting female suffrage on June 19, 1915, and the anniversary has been celebrated ever since; a special publication under the name June 19, dealing with issues of women's equality, appears on that day every year. The first female member of parliament was elected in 1922.

## Growing Patriotism

In the years before the First World War a strong national awakening took place among the Icelandic people. Farmers' unions, women's clubs, youth societies and countless other groups saw scope for improvement in all areas of Icelandic life and certainly achieved some success in the projects they undertook. The youth society movement was brought to Iceland from Norway early in the century. After the first youth society was established in Akureyri in 1906, branches spread rapidly all over the country, working for a popular national and cultural awakening under the motto: Educate the people, cultivate the land. Their activities included sport, cultural events and afforestation work. They were also active campaigners for the introduction of a national flag, embracing poet Einar Benediktsson's idea for a white cross on a blue background. Although Iceland eventually adopted a slightly different design, a red and white cross on a blue background, the blue-white flag has been the symbol of the youth societies and their national federation ever since.

## The Draft Constitution of 1908

Christian IX, the King who brought Iceland the constitution in 1874, died in 1906. He was succeeded by his son, Frederick VIII, who along with many influential Danes was eager to improve relations with Iceland. A group of Icelandic parliamentarians was invited to Denmark in 1906 and the King visited his subjects in

*From the Danish King's*
*visit of 1907.*

Iceland in 1907, accompanied by several distinguished Danish politicians. The same year the King appointed a new committee of Danish and Icelandic politicians to review the union of these two countries and the political ties between them. Both Hannes Hafstein, the minister of Iceland, and I. C. Christensen, prime minister of Denmark, were on the committee, and after settling their initial differences they drew up proposals that met most of the Icelanders' wishes. One of the Icelandic delegates, Skúli Thoroddsen, complained that the draft failed to secure Iceland's constitutional status well enough, but his proposed amendment received no support.

The draft declared that Iceland was a free and independent country. Iceland and Denmark would have the same King, and pursue a common policy in certain external respects such as foreign and military affairs, supervision of territorial waters and use of the Danish national flag abroad. The supreme court in Copenhagen would remain the highest court for Iceland, and several other areas of activity were entrusted to Danish administration until otherwise determined. Either nation would be empowered to demand a review of the treaty after twenty-five years, while all common responsibilities except the civil list and foreign and military affairs would be discontinued after ten years if desired.

When the draft constitution was announced in Iceland it was generally well received in the beginning, but doubts soon emerged about its merits. In the heated debate that followed, various political leaders eventually turned against it. Fervent agitation on the draft constitution issue dominated the general election in the summer of 1908, when its opponents scored a heavy victory and it was rejected. One factor contributing to the defeat dealt out in this memorable election might have been the fact that a secret ballot was used for the first time, but the crucial point was that a great majority would not longer tolerate any compromise with Denmark.

When the Althing gathered in the autumn, minister Hannes Hafstein presented the draft constitution as a bill, but since he only enjoyed a minority in the house after losing the election he had no hope of getting it through. The majority responded with a vote of no confidence and Hannes Hafstein resigned from office, thereby establishing a democratic tradition. It can be taken for granted that Hannes Hafstein and the other Icelandic committee members had won as much as the Danes were prepared to concede in negotiations at that time, but this did not help. The majority preferred gaining nothing at all to striking a compromise.

*Minister Björn Jónsson.*

## Björn Jónsson, Minister 1909–1911

While Hannes Hafstein and other supporters of the draft constitution belonged to the Home Rule Party, its opponents established a new political group which they called the Independence Party. Obliged to name a successor as minister, they could not decide among four candidates: Björn Jónsson, Hannes Thorsteinsson, Kristján Jónsson and Skúli Thoroddsen. The issue was settled by a vote in which Björn Jónsson emerged as winner and duly went to Denmark, where the King appointed him to the office of minister for Iceland. His party had a solid majority at the time, but did not take long to split into several factions. Many of the new minister's actions incurred the disapproval or even outright opposition of his own party members, for instance his expulsion of Tryggvi Gunnarsson, director of the National Bank, from office without warning and without specific reason. Mass protests and demonstrations resulted, and many of his former supporters left the party too, claiming he was not tough enough towards the Danish authorities. In a short while he had lost his parliamentary majority and after a vote of no confidence he was compelled to resign. The King then appointed Kristján Jónsson as minister and he served in that office from 1911 to 1912.

In the meantime, certain constitutional amendments had been passed, including changes in electoral rights and the abolition of royal appointment of members to the Althing, which meant that parliament had to be dissolved and a new election called. The Home Rule Party won a firm victory and regained its majority in the Althing, and Hannes Hafstein became minister for the second time.

Björn Jónson's ministry had been a rather tragic affair and met an abrupt end. After a long and distinguished career as a newspaper editor and politician, he became minister as an old man in poor health and probably failed to live up to the expectations that his supporters had of him in that office. He died in 1912.

## Constitutional Amendments and the Flag

Hannes Hafstein was minister of Iceland for the second time between 1912 and 1914. He enjoyed a commanding majority in parliament, with thirty-one out of forty members. The Home Rule Party and the Independence Party united in a new alliance which they called the Union Party and set as its main task to work towards a satisfactory solution to the question of relations with Denmark. In opposition were more radical members who wanted to sever ties with Denmark for good and claimed that the Union Party's approach was far too slow.

Hannes Hafstein reintroduced the draft constitution from 1908, altering it in some respects in deference to public opinion. But the Danish authorities refused to

*The controversial blue and white flag on a boat in Reykjavík harbour, before being confiscated.*

make any further concessions, feeling the Icelanders had shown ingratitude by rejecting the draft from 1908. King Frederick VIII died in 1912 and was succeeded by his son, Christian X, who was considered more conservative towards Iceland than his father had been. The Danes now offered to discuss the question on the basis of the constitutional law of 1871, and did not make as sweeping concessions as they had in the 1908 draft. But in spite of Danish stubbornness, Hannes Hafstein succeeded in securing some amendments to the constitution in 1913, including wider electoral rights and the abolition of royal appointments to parliament.

In 1913 public opinion was shaken by an incident in Reykjavík. A young man who had been rowing his boat in the harbour had hoisted the blue and white Icelandic flag, but was apprehended by a Danish coastguard vessel and had his flag confiscated, on the grounds that only the red and white Danish flag might be hoisted at sea. The incident created a major stir and was considered a great insult towards the national feelings of the Icelanders.

The national flag question was raised in the Althing but agreement could not be reached on the blue and white one, because some members claimed it resembled the Greek flag too closely. A resolution was passed that Iceland should have its own flag at home and on ships within territorial limits. The King agreed, provided the flag was not too similar to that of any other country. A committee appointed by Hannes Hafstein ruled that the blue and white design was in fact too reminiscent of the Greek flag and proposed a blue, red and white one instead. In parliament a majority voted for the blue and white flag as their first choice, and the three colours as an alternative, and left the decision to the King. In 1915, the King decreed that it should be blue, red and white, which has been the design of the national flag of Iceland ever since.

Hannes Hafstein had not succeeded in winning a repeal of the law that obliged all Icelandic affairs to be referred to the Danish council of state before taking effect. After the 1914 election he resigned on the grounds of uncertain parliamentary support, and Sigurdur Eggerz was chosen to become minister in his place and duly appointed by the King. His main task was to win approval for certain constitutional changes and the national flag, but when the King would not agree to his reservations concerning the constitution, he resigned from office in 1915. The King then appointed one of the younger leaders of the Independence Party, Einar Arnórsson, as minister and he served in that office until 1917. He saw the national flag issue safely home, and secured amendments including electoral rights for women, but avoided tackling the constitutional reservation about the Danish council of state, which remained deadlocked. But political divisions had begun to change. In 1916 two new parties were formed, the Social Democratic Party and the Progressive Party, while the old parties split in several directions. In 1917, lacking support in parliament, Einar Arnórsson resigned. A strong government had become imperative to handle the difficult situation created by the World War, and as there was no clear majority it was decided to form a coalition government with three ministers: Jón Magnússon from the Home Rule Party was prime minister and the Independence Party and the Progressive Party had one minister each.

*Sigurdur Eggerz, minister 1914-15 and prime minister 1922-24*

*Einar Arnórsson minister 1915-17.*

## Iceland and World War I

During World War I, from 1914 to 1918, Iceland had widespread difficulties to contend with. Contact with Denmark was limited by military activity, which forced the Icelanders to become increasingly self-reli-

*Reykjavík harbour froze solid during the harsh winter of 1918.*

ant. In a sense the war was an instructive event for the Icelanders, teaching them to think and act more independently as a nation. The war even had some outright benefits, for example for fishing. Foreign trawlers stopped sailing to Iceland to fish, leaving local fleets alone in command of the catch. Demand for fish and other products from Iceland grew abroad, and prices boomed, especially in the first two or three years. Shipping companies and export manufacturers reaped the benefits, but prices of imported goods rose too. Since wages remained more or less the same, working people reacted to their increasing hardship with political action and strikes. Labour unions grew stronger, and in the middle of the war, in 1916, formed a national federation.

In wartime, Iceland benefited enormously from having its own merchant fleet and being able to trade directly where business was best, for instance in Great Britain and the United States, without going through Danish middlemen any longer. But near the end of 1916 the situation worsened, when the British forced Iceland to sell them all their export products at fixed prices, in order to prevent them ending up in German hands. Early in 1917 the Germans began unrestricted submarine warfare, causing serious problems for ships in the Iceland traffic and even sinking some of them. Goods became scarce as a result, which fuelled inflation and also struck at basic industries by depriving them of necessary supplies such as coal and salt for fisheries. The allied powers had great need of ships and because of the troubles in the fishing industry Iceland sold a large part of its trawler fleet to France in 1917, in answer to an allied demand and for a fair price. That year, too, growing shortages forced Iceland to introduce widespread rationing. The government tried to help the situation by setting up a state-run trading company which soon took over most of the import trade, much to the annoyance of the merchants. Compounding the other difficulties, high unemployment followed the sale of so many ships, and the government launched a job creation programme to alleviate the situation, for example by starting lignite mining in the west and north.

The terribly severe winter of 1917–1918 was one of the coldest on record. The cold weather was accompanied by drift ice which blocked the coasts and caused extensive crop failures and damage to pasture. In autumn 1918 there was a gigantic eruption in the volcano Katla, which also caused damage to farming land in many parts of the country. About the same time an epidemic of exceptionally dangerous Spanish influenza swept the country, with many fatalities, so political difficulties were not the only problem that the Icelandic people faced on the road to independence.

### The Act of Union with Denmark, 1918

When the coalition government was formed in 1917 its main task was supposed to be to bring the political dispute with Denmark to a satisfactory conclusion. Outside Iceland, national self-determination had been accepted as a valid political principle and the Icelanders felt that the same rule should apply to them in relation to Denmark. At this juncture it proved useful that the Danes themselves were in a similar situation. They were trying to get Germany to cede North Schleswig, basing their demands on the right to self-determination of the inhabitants there. Germany had taken this land from Denmark in the war of 1864, but the population was largely Danish. After some negotiations and a local plebiscite, the region was given back to Denmark.

Prime Minister Jón Magnússon started negotiations with the Danish authorities in 1917, and in 1918 the two sides agreed to appoint a parliamentary commiss-

*Jón Magnússonn, prime minister 1917-22 and 1924-26.*

ion to find a solution satisfactory to both. The Danish commissioners arrived in Iceland at the end of June 1918 and worked for weeks with their Icelandic colleagues. After initial difficulties caused by the strong conservatism of some Danish representatives, who refused to entertain any major changes in relations between the two countries, they gradually yielded and an agreement was finally reached about the future arrangement. This new union treaty was then ratified by the respective parliaments in Denmark and Iceland, and confirmed in a national referendum in Iceland by a vast majority. On the last day of November the King ratified the union act and on December 1, 1918, the free and independent Icelandic Kingdom was proclaimed with a ceremony in Reykjavík when the Danish flag was lowered from the government building and the Icelandic flag hoisted to the top.

In the union act Iceland was at last acknowledged as a sovereign and independent state. The first paragraph was the most important and read: Denmark and Iceland are both free and independent countries and in union with the one and same King and the other principles on which they agree in this act. The treaty stipulated that Icelanders and Danes should have mutual rights of citizenship, Denmark should take care of Iceland's foreign affairs and guard its territorial waters until the Icelanders wished to take over, and that the supreme court in Copenhagen should serve as the highest court for Iceland until Iceland had established its own supreme court. The treaty was to be valid for the next twenty-five years, until 1943. Either the Danish or Icelandic parliament was allowed to demand a review of the treaty by 1940, and if no new treaty had been made at the wish of either or both nations by 1943, it would automatically be revoked. This clause was cited in 1944 when all ties with Denmark were severed and the republic proclaimed.

The union act of 1918 was a great victory for Iceland and that year will always be counted as one of the most remarkable in the history of the nation. It brought the Icelandic people their independence at last, and with it began the era of the sovereign Icelandic Kingdom.

# The Icelandic Kingdom 1918–1944

## December 1, Independence Day

The union treaty with Denmark went into effect on December 1, 1918, and was marked by a solemn ceremony and festivities in Reykjavík. Ministers of the government and presidents of the Althing honoured the memory of Jón Sigurdsson by placing flowers on his grave. A massive crowd gathered in front of the government building to hear Sigurdur Eggerz, one of the ministers, give a speech on this magnificent occasion. At noon the Danish flag on the government house was lowered and the Icelandic flag hoisted to the top as a symbol of independence. This was followed by speeches, music, greetings from foreign states and a holy service in the cathedral.

The independence celebration was a quiet and very solemn occasion, where people showed their happiness in a restrained and respectful manner. A great victory had been won and the whole nation rejoiced.

## Sovereignty in Reality

In 1920 a new constitution for the Kingdom of Iceland took effect. Legislation and other important governmental decisions were considered in the cabinet council of Iceland, thereby confirming the separation of Denmark and Iceland in reality at last. Before long, Iceland took over the duties which Denmark had temporarily dispatched on its behalf according to the union treaty. A supreme court for Iceland was established in 1920, the Icelandic coastguard service started in part as early as 1922, and the foreign service was taken over by Icelanders in stages. The first Icelandic embassy abroad was established in Copenhagen in 1920 with Sveinn Björnsson as ambassador, and Denmark opened its embassy in Reykjavík the same year. Sovereignty became clear in most respects. The country had, for instance, its own civil rights and its own currency, the Icelandic Króna. Among other promul-

*Salting of herring, one of the main industries of the 1920s.*

gations by this new state was a declaration of perpetual neutrality in military conflicts in the world.

### Economic Growth

After the end of World War I in 1918 Iceland went through a difficult period, like the world in general. There were economic troubles with unstable markets, price slumps, currency devaluations and mounting foreign debts. But after 1924 a considerable recovery took place and the situation remained fairly favourable until 1930, when the Great Depression which started in the United States in autumn 1929 began to spread around the world. One of its first major casualties in Iceland was the Bank of Iceland, which collapsed in 1930, although the Fisheries Bank was established on its ruins. Another new bank, also state-owned, the Agricultural Bank, had also been set up in 1929.

Fishing was a growth industry after the war. Many new steam trawlers and other fishing vessels were bought after 1920 to replace those sold during the war and to bolster the fleet. The old sail-powered decked vessels disappeared for the most part over this period and were replaced by motorized ships. The herring industry which the Norwegians had built up in the east and north was taken over by Icelanders, and Siglu-fjördur in the north became the main harbour and centre for herring almost right up until the stock's virtual collapse after the middle of the twentieth century. Fish processing became increasingly mechanized in this period. The first large freezing plant was established in Reykjavík in 1930; six years later, six had been built and in 1944 there were sixty-two freezing plants spread all over the country. Although fish was quick-frozen to a large extent for export, the old preservation techniques of drying and salting were still widely used to meet demand in individual markets.

Change and technological innovation also swept the countryside. Farmers began irrigating the land to increase the hay yield, and the two largest irrigation systems were established in 1923 and 1927 in the southern lowlands. Bigger crops of grass for haymaking allowed production to be stepped up, which was backed up by construction of large abattoirs and meat-freezing plants, while the old dairy farms were replaced by mechanized dairy centres, the largest of which operates in Selfoss and dates back to 1929. Manifold technological innovations and improvements enabled farmers to drain wet, marshy land and use imported fertilizers to cultivate their fields for fodder, instead of the traditional mowing of outfields or meadows. Farmers were supported in many ways by new legislation such as the agricultural law of 1923 and sale and

*Salting and drying of cod, a traditional preservation technique.*

management law of 1935. Nonetheless, infectious diseases of sheep proved a recurrent problem, brought in with an imported foreign breed.

In spite of improvements and progress in agriculture, the population drift from the countryside and into towns and villages gained momentum. In 1920 about 40% of the population were engaged in farming, in 1940 about 33% and in 1970 only 14%. In towns and villages various new industries were set up to help Iceland become self-sufficient in more products and provide work for a growing number of people.

## New Methods in Communications

*Unchanged for centuries, farming methods began to change early last century.*

Marine communications increased rapidly after the war years as the Iceland Steamship Company and other enterprises expanded their fleets to maintain shipping services to and from the country. A coastal liner company was established in 1922 by the government to connect the tiny communities scattered all around Iceland. Sea transport was of vital importance before the advent of roads and automobiles, and all communications on land were very primitive at this time. When plans for building railways came to nothing, the only way to improve land communications was to build more and better roads and bridges. That is what was done, but it was a long process. In 1924 there were about 300 automobiles in the country,

*The first automobile in Iceland, wich arrived in 1904.*

mostly in Reykjavík, but only a very few short roads existed outside the town. The drivers of this time, however, were like explorers, constantly striving to cover greater distances, and thereby marking the sites for future roads. These pioneers recorded many triumphs of endeavour, one of the greatest being the first car journey from Borgarnes in the south (which was linked to Reykjavík by ferry at the time) to the main town of Akureyri in the north in 1928. Serviceable roads spread rapidly all over the country and the number of lorries and cars grew every year, although private cars did not become commonplace until after the middle of the century.

Aviation started relatively early in Iceland, as the first Icelandic airline was founded in 1919, a short-lived venture with a single plane. Experiments continued and a number of flights were made between 1928 and 1930. The first plane from abroad landed in Iceland in 1924 when the Nelson expedition from the United States stopped over. In 1930 a Zeppelin arrived, and again in 1931. In 1933 Balbo's Italian flying squadron landed in Iceland, and Charles Lindbergh did the same on an Atlantic crossing.

In 1937 the Akureyri Airways Company was established and operated regular flights between Akureyri and Reykjavík. By the following year it had already moved to Reykjavík and changed its name to Icelandair. Another airline, Loftleidir, was established in 1944, and both introduced scheduled international flights to and from Iceland after World War II. These two companies were to merge into a new Icelandair much later, in 1973.

## *Politics in the Inter-War Years*

When the dispute with Denmark about freedom and independence was nearing its conclusion, Iceland's political emphases and divisions shifted. The old parties dissolved and their successors focused more closely on economic and domestic affairs, like the Social Democratic Party and the Progressive Party, both established in 1916.

Jón Magnússon's first coalition government lasted from 1917 to 1919, when he formed a new coalition until 1922. He belonged to the old Home Rule Party which was now fading away as new parties took shape on the right wing. In 1922 Sigurdur Eggerz from the old Independence Party formed a coalition government until 1924. That year saw what was left of the Home Rule Party and the Independence Party unite, along with other groups, to form the new Conservative Party. Some of the home rulers had moved over to the Progressive Party, and a faction of the Independence Party split into the Citizens' Party and the Liberal Party. There were other factions still, and enormous political confusion reigned on the right until 1929, when the Conservative and Liberal Parties united in a new Independence Party which absorbed them all,

*Aeroplanes came first to Iceland in 1919.*

and has been the largest political party in Iceland ever since.

Jón Magnússon became the first leader of the Conservative Party in 1924 and the same year he formed a new single-party government. On his death in 1926, Jón Thorláksson succeeded him as leader and prime minister until an election defeat in 1927. Jón Thorláksson remained leader of the Conservative Party and later the Independence Party until 1934, when Ólafur Thors took over the leadership.

*Jón Thorláksson, prime minister 1926-27.*

After the Conservatives had lost the 1927 election, the Progressive Party, led by Tryggvi Thórhallsson, formed a new government with the support of the Social Democratic Party. Prime Minister Thórhallsson was an influential man, but even more influential was his minister of culture and justice, Jónas Jónsson. This government's term of office, from 1927 to 1931, was a period of great progress with intense action to stimulate culture and industry. Schools and cultural institutions were established, roads and bridges built in all parts of the country, and coastal shipping increased. Work began on the National Theatre and other public buildings, the State Hospital in Reykjavík was opened in 1930, herring factories were built, farms modernized and a new bank established to support the agricultural sector, along with many other measures.

This government ran aground in 1931 when the Social Democrats withdrew after demanding electoral reforms. The Social Democrats and Independents started talks about a new division into a few large constituencies, and proportional representation. But before they could force a vote of no confidence in the government, Prime Minister Tryggvi Thórhallsson dissolved parliament and called a new election. Despite outraged protests from the opposition and mass demonstrations against him, the prime minister had a legal right to do so, and in the 1931 election the Progressive Party won a majority of seats from the prevailing arrangement of constituencies, even though it earned only about 36% of the votes. Tryggvi Thórhallsson formed a single-party government, but stepped down as party leader in 1932, when his successor

*Tryggvi Thórhallsson, prime minister 1927-32.*

Ásgeir Ásgeirsson took the Progressive Party into coalition with the Independence Party. These two parties then introduced sweeping constituency reforms which established the electoral structure for a long time to come. Under the new system, twenty members were elected from one-man district constituencies, twelve from six two-man constituencies and six from Reykjavík, with the remaining eleven seats allocated among parties as a weighting factor to bring their representation in parliament in line with their respective share of the votes at a national level. At the same time the voting age was lowered from twenty-five to twenty-one.

These changes to the constitution called for two general elections to be held in 1933 and 1934 and in this political turmoil the Progressive Party split and a breakaway faction formed the Farmers' Party, which gained a few seats in parliament but disappeared after 1937. Tryggvi Thórhallsson left to lead the new party, but lost in the election against Hermann Jónasson, the future Progressive Party leader.

Hermann Jónasson led the Progressives into a new coalition in 1934 with the Social Democrats. Calling itself the Government of the Working Classes, its achievements included the establishment of comprehensive health care and a general public insurance system in 1936, which has lasted, with countless modifications, to the present day. Hermann Jónasson led this government until 1939 when he formed a new and broader coalition, known as the National Government, comprising the Progressive, Social Democratic and Independence Parties. Only the three members of the Socialist Party remained in opposition, and the government was effectively able to ignore them. Under this new coalition the number of ministers was increased from three to five.

The idea behind this broad coalition was to create a strong government to cope with a major economic crisis, and it was the brainchild of Jónas Jónsson, who led the Progressive Party until 1944 when Hermann Jónasson succeeded him (even when party leader, Jónas Jónsson never served as prime minister). The National Government fell in 1942 when the Social Democ-

149

*One of the first hydroelectric generators set up in Iceland.*

rats pulled out following disagreement over economic policies and its new demands for constituency reform. Some changes were instituted, such as increasing the number of parliamentary seats from forty-nine to fifty-two, and the need to ratify this amendment to the constitution meant that two elections were held in 1942, with Ólafur Thors forming a minority Independence Party caretaker government between them. Attempts to form a new government after the second election ended in deadlock and in the end the regent, Sveinn Björnsson, appointed a non-parliamentary government with Björn Thórdarson as prime minister, which remained in office until after the proclamation of the Republic in 1944.

The Social Democratic Party and labour movement were closely connected in the beginning and maintained a smooth relationship for years. But in 1930 a radical faction broke away to establish the Communist Party of Iceland under the leadership of Brynjólfur Bjarnason and Einar Olgeirsson. Their number of followers was small at first but grew during the Depression and the party finally won three seats in parliament in 1937. Many leftists dreamt of uniting these two socialist parties. Hédinn Valdemarsson of the Social Democrats made an attempt to do so, but was then expelled from his own party. Along with defecting Social Democrats and the Communists, he formed a new party under the name of the United Socialist

*Hermann Jónasson prime minister 1934-42 and 1956-58.*

*Socialist leader Einar Olgeirsson.*

People's Party. Although Héðinn Valdemarsson soon came to dislike its pro-Russian leanings and left, the party lived on and grew with time.

Of other foreign political doctrines of the period, a national socialist movement sprang up, under the influence of Adolf Hitler. In 1933 a Nazi Party was founded in Reykjavík and had some followers elsewhere too. It was a noisy group, but never numerous. Part of it was later incorporated into the Independence Party, and what was left faded into quiet extinction in the next few years.

## The Millennial Festival of the Althing (1930)

The Icelandic Parliament or Althing had been founded in AD930 and lasted without interruption thereafter, apart from the interval from 1800 to 1843. Its millennium was celebrated with a festival at Thingvellir from June 26 to 28, 1930, at which an estimated 35,000 people gathered. In addition to the national festival at Thingvellir there were many other similar celebrations all around the country during the summer.

On this festive occasion, Iceland was honoured in many ways with gifts, congratulatory wishes and visits by representatives of governments of many other countries and other noble guests. The noblest of them all was the King, Christian X, who made an official state visit with his queen and retinue to celebrate with his subjects and honour one of the oldest parliaments in the world.

## Depression and Riots

Like all its neighbouring countries, Iceland suffered badly during the Great Depression in the 1930s. Export markets became unstable and prices there plummeted, and bankruptcies were commonplace. The consequence was growing poverty, unemployment and stagnation. The authorities tried to meet these difficulties by restricting imports and stimulating domestic industries and production. Special aid was granted to agriculture and fisheries after 1933, and although

*The millennial festival of the Althing was celebrated in 1930 at Thingvellir.*

this helped a good deal, massive economic hardship characterized the decade. Government bodies tried to alleviate the situation by increasing public works such as road-making and construction of bridges, schools and other buildings, and of hydroelectric power plants. The first big power station on the river Sog in the south was opened in 1937, and in the north the river Laxá power plant was completed in 1939.

In some places, especially in Reykjavík, the authorities tried to create jobs for the unemployed in such areas as trench digging, snow clearance and the like. But funds were limited and in 1932 Reykjavík municipal council announced plans to cut wages for such jobs. Workers protested and the police were called in to stop the demonstrations. The workers then turned against the police and a pitched battle ensued, in which many people were seriously injured before the police quelled the riot. In a sense, the workers had won, for their wages were not cut afterwards, and the state supported the city authorities in continuing the job-creation programme.

## Growing Culture and Art

*Painter
Jóhannes S. Kjarval.*

*Poet Steinn Steinarr.*

Cultural activity flourished in Iceland in the first half of the century. Poets and writers were numerous, and much pioneering work was done in other artistic fields. The best-known lyrical poets of the period were Stefán Sigurdsson (1887–1933), Davíd Stefánsson (1895–1964), Jóhannes Jónasson (1899–1972), Tómas Gudmundsson (1901–1983), Gudmundur Bödvarsson (1904–1974), and finally Steinn Steinarr (1908–1958) who was a pioneer in a new modernist lyrical genre whose influence has been pervasive in the latter half of the century.

Among novelists, Halldór Laxness (1902–1998) was by far the most renowned, especially after he won the Nobel Prize for Literature in 1955. But there were many other excellent writers, like Thórbergur Thórdarson (1889–1974, Gudmundur G. Hagalín (1898–1985) and Gudmundur Daníelsson (1910–1990), to name only a few. Some Icelandic authors of this period wrote in Danish or other foreign languages to reach a wider audience abroad, for instance playwrights Jóhann Sigurjónsson (1880–1919) and Gudmundur Kamban (1888–1945) and novelists Jón Sveinsson, or Nonni, (1857–1944), Gunnar Gunnarsson (1888–1975) and Kristmann Gudmundsson (1901–1982).

Painting attracted more and more artists. Thórarinn B. Thorláksson (1867–1924) was one of the first, and among the legion who followed in his footsteps were Ásgrímur Jónsson (1876–1958), Jóhannes S. Kjarval (1885–1972), Jón Stefánsson (1881–1962) and Finnur Jónsson (1892–1994). Among sculptors the best known were Einar Jónsson (1874–1954) and Ásmundur Sveinsson (1893–1983).

Music flourished too; music schools were established in Reykjavík and other towns, and public participation in choirs and instrumental performances ran high all over the country. The Iceland Symphony Orchestra was eventually founded in 1950. There were several composers too, like Bjarni Thorsteinsson (1861–1938) and Jón Leifs (1899–1965). Drama became very popular after the Reykjavík Theatre Comp-

*Writer Gunnar
Gunnarsson*

*Writer and Nobel Prize winner in 1955 Halldór Laxness and his wife Audur Sveinsdóttir.*

any was founded on 1897, and the National Theatre opened in Reykjavík in 1950. Films came to Reykjavík in the first years of the century and cinemas have operated regularly since 1906. A private radio station opened in Reykjavík in 1926, but did not last long. The State Broadcasting Service began in 1930 and soon reached a nationwide audience.

## Iceland and World War II

On September 1, 1939, Hitler invaded Poland and World War II began. For the first few months it had little direct effect on Iceland, although the public keenly followed its development and widespread sympathies were expressed for the Poles when they were attacked from both sides, and with the Finns during the Winter War of 1939–1940.

Germany had shown considerable interest in Iceland for some years, as had been clearly shown with numerous visits, expeditions and other gestures. German agents had studied possible facilities for ships and aircraft and cultivated connections and supporters in the country, for instance within the Icelandic Nazi movement. In these years it took a certain amount of courage to reject "friendly" requests from this major power, but that is precisely what Iceland did in 1939 when Prime Minister Hermann Jónasson refused the Germans landing permission for their Lufthansa aircraft.

The effect of the war was first felt clearly in Iceland when the Germans occupied Denmark and Norway after a lightning attack on April 9, 1940. Iceland thereby lost all contact with Denmark and the King was no longer able to fulfil his royal duties towards the country. The day after the German invasion of Denmark, Iceland's parliament decided that the government should take over all the duties and functions of the King, along with all foreign relations and the supervision of territorial waters, which in accordance with the Union Treaty of 1918 had officially been in Danish hands, although the Icelanders had in fact largely controlled them for years.

### The British Occupation of Iceland (1940)

After the German occupation of Denmark and Norway in April 1940, Britain secretly informed the Icelandic government that it thought that Iceland might be in danger, and that the British would use any means to prevent Iceland suffering the same fate. Because of its location in the middle of the North Atlantic, Iceland was of great strategic importance, as the earlier, rejected German request for landing permits had shown. Fearing that the Germans would establish military bases in Iceland, the British decided to move first, sending a large force to occupy both Iceland and the Faroe Islands at the same time. Troops landed in

Reykjavík early in the morning of May 10, 1940, and took full control of the country in a very short time. The Icelandic government protested strongly against this violation of the nation's neutrality, but there was little more that an unarmed country could do. On the evening of May 10, the prime minister broadcast an address to the Icelandic nation in which he repeated the protests against the violation, but asked people to keep calm, regard the British soldiers as guests in their country and treat them accordingly. The British, for their part, declared they would not interfere in Icelandic affairs and would leave as soon as they could.

The arrival of the British troops wrought a rapid, radical and irreversible change upon life in Iceland. Commerce of all kinds boomed, and work was available for virtually everybody constructing barracks and other buildings, roads, airfields and other facilities for the forces. The great demand for manpower caused wages to rise rapidly and unemployment disappeared almost overnight. Industry flourished, of course, and general living standards rose. Most of the troops were stationed in Reykjavík and the south, but there were also considerable numbers in and around Akureyri and in the east and west, meaning that their presence was felt everywhere. The occupation brought work and money, removing the legacy of the Depression quickly and almost completely.

## Americans Replace the British

The British stood very much alone against Germany after the fall of France in 1940. At the same time the United States was neutral in the war, although it supported and helped Britain in many ways. To lighten the war burden somewhat, the Americans took over the defence of Iceland in the summer of 1941. Iceland agreed, on condition that the Americans withdrew all their forces as soon as the war was over, acknowledged the independence of Iceland in all respects and procured the same recognition from other states. When the president of the United States assented to

*Barracks in Reykjavík.*

these terms, the defence treaty was passed by Iceland's parliament. With this treaty, the earlier declaration of Iceland's perpetual neutrality was effectively abolished.

The first American forces arrived on July 7, 1941. Better funded and equipped than the British forces, they brought even more work to do for them, and with it, more money. In addition, the Americans brought in equipment such as bulldozers, cranes and jeeps which few Icelanders had seen before but would soon adopt for their own development work. Bilateral trade with the USA began to soar.

Relations with the foreign armed forces were good in general. Inevitably some friction arose, but not to the extent that might have been expected, bearing in mind that they were probably half as many as the whole population of Iceland. During the war, Iceland's exports fetched high prices, especially fish products. But at the same time, heavy fatalities were suffered when fishing and merchant vessels were sunk at sea. Iceland actually lost a larger percentage of its total population owing to the war than, for instance, the Americans.

## The Union Treaty Revoked

Once the Icelandic authorities had taken over all duties of the King after ties with Denmark were suddenly cut by the German invasion in April 1940, parliament began discussing the Union Treaty. It reached the conclusion that Iceland had acquired the absolute right to sever these ties, since Denmark had not been able to perform the duties it had undertaken towards Iceland in the Union Treaty of 1918, and that Iceland would have to take them over. Furthermore, parliament concluded that the Union Treaty of 1918 with Denmark would not be renewed or prolonged.

Afterwards, in the early spring of 1941, parliament decided to choose a regent for one year at a time to act as sovereign and carry out the royal duties which the Icelandic government had taken into its own hands after the German invasion of Denmark. Finally, parliament concluded that a republic should be proclaimed in Iceland as soon as the Union Treaty with Denmark had been formally revoked. Accordingly, parliament elected as regent Sveinn Björnsson, former ambassador to Denmark, on June 17, 1941, and he took power as sovereign in the country from the same time.

The political situation was rather troubled at this time. In 1942, there were long and serious strikes for higher wages. When the majority parties in government tried to control the economic situation with arbitrary legislation, the Social Democrats walked out. The Progressive and Independence Parties sat on, but would soon fall when the Social Democrats put forward demands for constituency reforms. Because this involved a change to the constitution, two general elections had to be held in 1942. The political balance of power had shifted sharply, and after the second election the Socialist Party had grown to hold ten out of the fifty-two seats in parliament, the Social Democratic Party had seven, the Independence Party twenty and the Progressive Party fifteen. As none of the parties had a majority in parliament, they tried to negotiate about some sort of coalition, but after two months of deadlock, regent Sveinn Björnsson formed a non-political government with Björn Thórdarson as prime minister.

Public and party political opinion was divided about how quickly the ties with Denmark should be cut. Some loyalists thought it more favourable, and polite, to defer this decision until Denmark was free again and then negotiate on equal terms, but this view was not widely supported. Early in 1944, parliament ruled that the Union Treaty with Denmark was revoked. This conclusion was then ratified in a national referendum in the early spring by 97.35% of the votes. Afterwards only a handful of formalities remained before the Republic of Iceland could be proclaimed on June 17, 1944.

# The Republic of Iceland

## The Proclamation of the Republic, 1944

The Icelandic people's dream of full freedom and independence was at last realized under the shadow of World War II. At a solemn meeting on June 16, the Althing concluded that the Union Treaty with Denmark was revoked and that a new constitution of the Republic of Iceland should take effect on June 17, 1944. A crowd estimated at 25,000 gathered at the old parliament site of Thingvellir the day after. The prime minister opened the ceremony, then the bishop gave a blessing and choirs sang two psalms. This was followed by a short parliamentary session, at which the speaker of the Althing, Gísli Sveinsson, declared that the constitution of the Republic of Iceland had become valid. Then the flag of the Republic was hoisted on top of the old Law Rock and the bells in the church of Thingvellir and every other church around the country were rung simultaneously for two minutes. After one minute's silence, the national anthem sounded over the Parliament Plains.

Later in the day the first President of the Republic, in whom the ultimate executive power of this new state would be vested, was elected by parliament; subsequent presidents were to be chosen in a national election. Sveinn Björnsson, the former regent, was elected president, and delivered an address to the nation. Speeches and congratulations from foreign deputies followed, and late in the afternoon a telegram expressing good wishes arrived from King Christian X, who was hailed for this gesture, since the German occupation of Denmark had caused Iceland to part ways with him under exceptional circumstances. After these solemn ceremonies, a great national celebration was held at Thingvellir, with others taking place all over the country on June 17 and 18. The whole nation rejoiced heartily at what it saw as a major historical event, the fulfilment of freedom in the Republic.

## Presidents of the Republic

The new constitution of the Icelandic Republic took
effect on June 17, 1944, and was in most respects built
on the constitution of the Icelandic Kingdom. But
there was one major difference in that the President,
who now replaced the King, was to be chosen in a
general election for a four-year term of office at a time.
President Sveinn Björnsson (1881–1952) was chosen
by the parliament for the first time in 1944. In 1948
the first national presidential election was scheduled,
but since no other candidate stood, Sveinn Björnsson
was elected unopposed for a second term. He declared
Bessastadir the official residence of the Icelandic head
of state. This historic farm had served for centuries as
the headquarters of royal governors and other officials,
and had been recently bought by a wealthy man from
Reykjavík who donated the estate to the Icelandic
state. Sveinn Björnsson set the precedent for presidential protocol and traditions which have been broadly
continued by his successors, although each new in-
cumbent of the nation's highest office has inevitably
added an element of personal style.

President Sveinn Björnsson died in office late in the
winter of 1952, shortly before his second term was to
expire. Preparations began for the first national presidential election, which was fought by three candidates,

one of whom had the declared support of the two largest political parties in parliament. But this did not prove to be an asset, because popular opinion has always rejected all party political lines in the presidential elections. After a heated campaign, Ásgeir Ásgeirsson (1894–1972), former prime minister, won the election. He sat in office for four terms, and was always re-elected unopposed.

In 1968 Ásgeir Ásgeirsson announced that he would not seek re-election to office. Two candidates came forward, but no political parties were directly involved. After a hard-fought campaign, Kristján Eldjárn (1917–1981) won the election with about two-thirds of the votes. A former director of the National Museum, Kristján Eldjárn served as president for two more periods, and was re-elected unopposed.

In 1980, Kristján Eldjárn announced that he would not be seeking re-election to office, and four candidates were announced, three men and one woman. After a long and hard campaign, the female candidate, Vigdís Finnbogadóttir, former director of the Reykjavík Theatre, won the election, thereby becoming the first woman in the world to be elected head of state in a democratic election. She was elected unopposed in 1984 for a second term. In 1988 she faced a rival candidate and won a sweeping victory. In 1992 she was re-elected unopposed for a fourth term.

*Bessastadir residence of the President of Iceland.*

*The Presidents of Iceland.*
*Sveinn Björnsson, 1944-52.*
*Ásgeir Ásgeirsson, 1952-68.*
*Kristján Eldjárn, 1968-80,*
*Vigdís Finnbogadóttir,*
*1980-96,*
*Ólafur Ragnar Grímsson,*
*since 1996.*

Towards the end of 1995, President Vigdís Finnbogadóttir announced that after sixteen years in office she would not be standing again. An election was called and four candidates for the presidency came forward. After a hard campaign Ólafur Ragnar Grímsson won the election. Born in 1943, a former professor and politician, Ólafur Ragnar Grímsson took over the presidency on August 1, 1996 as Iceland's fifth president and has held the office since He was re-elected in 2000, 2004, 2008 and 2012, either with or without rival candidates.

All five presidents of the republic have earned universal honour and respect for the manner in which they have dispatched their duties, embodying the principles of national unity and Icelandic identity at home as well as abroad.

The constitution of the Icelandic Republic, as passed by parliament and ratified in a national referendum in 1944, was supposed to be reviewed soon afterwards.

*Ólafur Thors, prime minister 1942, 1944-47, 1949-50, 1953-56 and 1959-63.*

*Stefán Jóhann Stefánsson, prime minister 1947-49.*

*Steingrímur Steinþórsson, prime minister 1950-53.*

Several committees have worked on the matter, but no major changes have been made to date.

## Political Parties in the Republic

The party political delineations which emerged in the second and third decades of the last century have remained very much the same under the republic. There are the four major parties, the Social Democratic Party, the Progressive Party, the Independence Party and the Socialist Party, which later became the People's Alliance. Parties have split and new ones emerged, although most have proved short-lived. The National Defence Party won seats in parliament in 1953 and again in 1956, likewise the Union of Leftists and Liberals in 1971 and 1974, and the Social Democratic Alliance in 1983. The feminist Women's Alliance won seats in 1983, 1987 and 1991. The Citizens' Party entered parliament in 1987, and also the same year one member of the Regional Equality Party.

All this period, the Independence Party has been consistently the largest party with about 30–40% of the national vote. Reykjavík city was for years the political stronghold of the party, and with few exceptions it had a majority in the city council. But in the local elections of 1994 the former opposition parties formed an alliance and won a majority, and this happened again in 1998 and 2002. The leader of this alliance was Ingibjörg Sólrún Gísladóttir, who subsequently became mayor of Reykjavík. Tending right of centre in policy, the Independence Party mainly functions as a broad liberal party drawing support equally from all classes of society. It lost heavily but temporarily in 1987 when a splinter group set up the Citizens' Party. The leaders of the Independence Party under the republic have been Ólafur Thors, Bjarni Benediktsson, Jóhann Hafstein, Geir Hallgrímsson, Thorsteinn Pálsson, Davíð Oddsson, Geir Haarde and the current party leader, Bjarni Benediktsson (born 1970).

The Progressive Party lies somewhere in the political centre and originally was mostly supported by farmers and the cooperative movement. Over the

*Emil Jónsson, prime minister 1958-59.*

*Bjarni Benediktsson, prime minister 1963-70.*

*Jóhann Hafstein, prime minister 1970-71.*

past decades its support has grown in regional areas. The party has remained intact for the most part since 1934 with the exception of the Regional Equality Party breakaway in 1987. In general it has won about 20–25% of the national vote. Its leaders under the republic have been Hermann Jónsson, Eysteinn Jónsson, Ólafur Jóhannesson, Steingrímur Hermannsson, Halldór Ásgrímsson, Jón Sigurdsson (party leader), Gudni Ágústsson and the current leader, Sigmundur Davíd Gunnlaugsson.

The Socialist Party, later the People's Alliance, witnessed rapid growth in the war years, with influence in the government and the labour movement. Always a radical leftist party, it was often accused of excessive pro-Soviet sympathies, which was one reason why the rival National Defence Party was formed in 1953. A faction of the Social Democratic Party allied with the Socialist Party in the 1956 election, and the National Defence Party merged into it in 1963. This new fusion, called the People's Alliance, became a regular political party in 1968. In spite of some internal unrest, this party has held its ground with about 15–20% of the national vote. Under the republic, its leaders have been Einar Olgeirsson (in the Socialist Party) and, in the People's Alliance, Hannibal Valdemarsson, Ragnar Arnalds, Lúdvík Jósepsson, Svavar Gestsson, Ólafur Ragnar Grímsson and Margrét Frímannsdóttir.

The Social Democratic Party has had its ups and downs, with support swinging from under 10% up to 20%. It split in 1956 and much more seriously in 1983, but has recovered and reunited for the most part again. It was originally a workers' party drawing support mostly from the labour movement, but this was less the case later. Its leaders under the republic have been Stefán Jóhann Stefánsson, Hannibal Valdemarsson, Haraldur Gudmundsson, Emil Jónsson, Gylfi Th. Gíslason, Benedikt Gröndal, Kjartan Jóhannsson, Jón Baldvin Hannibalsson and Sighvatur Björgvinsson.

In the parliamentary election of 1999 three parties – the Socialists, Social Democrats and Women's Alliance – formed a coalition and won a good number of seats. Meanwhile, a faction of the People's Alliance broke away and formed a new party, the Left-Green Alliance, which also won seats The first leader of the

*Ólafur Jóhannesson, prime minister 1971-74 and 1978-79.*

*Geir Hallgrímsson, prime minister 1974-1978.*

*Benedikt Gröndal, prime minister 1979-1980.*

Left-Green Alliance was Steingrímur J Sigfússon He was followed by Katrín Jakobsdóttir. In 2000 the three leftist parties of the 1999 union merged to form a new party, the Coalition Party. The leaders of the old parties then resigned and a new chairman, Össur Skarphéd-insson, was chosen, later succeeded by Ingibjörg Sól-rún Gísladóttir, Jóhanna Sigurdardóttir and the current leader, Árni Páll Árnason In the election of 2003 this party won more seats and got 30% of the vote.

## Governments under the Republic

The main work of the Icelandic government during the war had focused on effecting the dissolution of the union with Denmark and the establishment of the Icelandic Republic. Since that time, serious economic questions and problems have increasingly occupied the respective governments. Iceland's political structure has not enabled any single party to govern alone, and the rule has been many varieties of coalition. The non-political government of 1942–1944 tried to tackle inflation and other economic problems, but lacked parliamentary support for its measures and resigned. Then it was time once again to form a parliamentary government.

Ólafur Thors began by taking his Independence Party into coalition with the Social Democratic Party and Socialist Party, to form the so-called Government of Reconstruction. Iceland had become relatively wealthy during the war and had extensive foreign currency reserves, and in late 1944 the government launched a comprehensive restoration and welfare programme. The plan involved moves to strengthen industries in various ways, the purchase of trawlers and other vessels from abroad, construction of herring factories and freezing plants, mechanization of agriculture, initiation of a social housing scheme, and much more. The Government of Reconstruction brought progress and prosperity in many ways, but when export prices fell and the foreign currency reserves were spent, the programme had to be slowed down. Among its many legislative achievements were a new social security and welfare act and education act in 1946. The government did not last until the end of

*Gunnar Thoroddsen,
prime minister
1980-1983.*

*Steingrímur Hermannsson,
prime minister
1983-87 and 1988-91.*

*Thorsteinn Pálsson,
prime minister
1987-88.*

1946, since the Socialists walked out to underline their opposition to the Keflavík base treaty with the USA.

It took some time to form a new coalition, which was led by Stefán Jóhann Stefánsson of the Social Democratic Party, together with the two large Independence and Progressive Parties. In office until 1949, it had major economic difficulties to contend with. By this time there were clear and strong reverberations from the Cold War, and the ruling parties strove to exclude the Socialists from all political influence. In 1949 the government lost its parliamentary majority when the Progressive Party refused to support its partners' economic measures. Ólafur Thors then formed a minority government with his Independence Party alone, promising measures to restore the economy including a hefty devaluation. The Progressive Party moved the first vote of no confidence to be made in parliament since 1911, and when it was endorsed by all parties except the Independents, Ólafur Thors resigned.

In 1950 a new coalition was formed by the Progressive Party and Independence Party, which lasted, with some changes, until 1956. Steingrímur Steinthórsson of the Progressives was prime minister until 1953, when Ólafur Thors took over. Milestones of its term of office were the extension of the fishery limit from three to four miles in 1952, and the bilateral defence agreement which allowed US forces to be stationed at the Keflavík base in 1951. This coalition had to tackle widespread economic problems and there were serious strikes in 1952 and 1955.

The Progressive Party left the government in 1956 and in the subsequent election formed an alliance with the Social Democrats. The alliance did not quite succeed in winning a majority but, with Hermann Jónasson as premier, formed a coalition with the People's Alliance, a leftist faction whose leader was Hannibal Valdemarsson. The government aimed to revoke the defence treaty with the USA and expel the US forces from the Keflavík base, but this plan was postponed after the Russian invasion of Hungary. Prime Minister Hermann Jónasson was forced to resign in 1958 when the labour movement refused to cooperate with the government on economic and counter-inflationary

*Davíð Oddsson, prime minister 1991-2004.*

*Halldór Ásgrímsson, prime minister 2004-06.*

*Geir Haarde, prime Minister 2006-2009.*

measures. This government extended the fishery limit from four to twelve miles in 1958.

The Independence and Social Democratic parties, who had begun discussing sweeping constituency reforms, formed a coalition under the premiership of Social Democrat Emil Jónsson. In 1959 the electoral reforms were passed in parliament and, since constitutional changes were involved, two elections had to be staged to ratify them. The Independence and Social Democratic parties won a majority and formed a coalition which lasted, with some changes, for twelve years and succeeded in establishing significant economic and political stability. Ólafur Thors was prime minister until 1963, when Bjarni Benediktsson took over until his death in 1970, and Jóhann Hafstein was premier until the coalition fell in the 1971 election.

Ólafur Jóhannesson of the Progressive Party took over the reins, in a coalition with the People's Alliance and the Union of Leftists and Liberals, which lasted until 1974. Among the issues it tackled were responses to the oil crisis, a devastating volcanic eruption on Heimaey in the Westman Islands, and the extension of the fishery limit from twelve to fifty miles. Eventually losing some of its parliamentary support, the government then called a new election.

After the 1974 election, Geir Hallgrímsson led the Independence Party into a coalition with the Progressive Party, which lasted until 1978 and was responsible for extending the territorial limit from 50 miles to the present 200 miles. After the 1978 election, the Progressive Party leader Ólafur Jóhannesson premiered a leftist coalition with the Social Democratic Party and the People's Alliance. That government soon fell when the Social Democrats walked out in 1979 and their leader Benedikt Gröndal headed a minority caretaker government which the Independence Party promised to maintain in office. After an election, the parties had still not agreed on a coalition when Gunnar Thoroddsen, deputy leader of the Independence Party, broke ranks and took a few of his party's members to join the Progressive Party and People's Alliance in a coalition, leaving the Independence Party

*Jóhanna Sigurdardóttir, prime minister 2009-2013, was the first woman to take that office.*

*Sigmundur Davíd Gunnlaugsson, prime minister since 2013.*

leadership in opposition. Besides the drama surrounding its formation, that government will largely be remembered for its currency reform, when the old króna, made nearly worthless by rampant inflation, was taken out of circulation and replaced by the new króna, at a rate of one to a hundred.

After the 1983 election Steingrímur Hermannsson formed a coalition between his Progressive Party and the Independence Party, which lasted until the 1987 election. The Independence Party split on the eve of that election and the breakaway Citizen' Party won enough seats to prevent any two-party coalition being formed. Thorsteinn Pálsson led his diminished Independence Party into a broad coalition with the Progressive and Social Democratic parties. It lasted only one year, when Thorsteinn Pálsson resigned after the parties failed to agree on economic questions. It was replaced by a coalition premiered by Steingrímur Hermannsson of the Progressive Party with the Social Democratic Party, People's Alliance and Regional Equality Party, which in 1990 strengthened its slender majority with the addition of some members of the Citizens' Party. The great achievement of that government was its virtual eradication of inflation with the joint support of employers and employees.

In 1991, the Independence Party, under the new leadership of Davíd Oddsson and with the Citizens' Party defectors almost all back under its wing, took office in a coalition with the Social Democratic Party. After the parliamentary election in 1995 Davíd Oddsson formed his second government, this time with the Progressive Party, and in 1999 he formed his third government, also with the Progressive Party. In the parliamentary election in 2003 these two parties, in spite of some loss of support, still won the majority of votes, whereupon Davíd Oddsson formed his fourth government, again with the Progressive Party. But in this case it was agreed that the chairman of the Progressive Party, Halldór Ásgrímsson, should take over as prime minister in the autumn of 2004. He remained in office until the summer of 2006 when the chairman of the Independence Party, Geir H. Haarde, took over as prime minister.

After the elections of 2007 and some losses in the Progressive Party, Geir Haarde, the leader of the Independence Party, formed a new government with the Coalition Party.

These last governments have worked for increased freedom in economic and industrial life and the privatization of formerly state-owned banks and other enterprises which have been sold to individuals or private companies.

## The Banking Collapse of 2008

In the first years of the twenty-first century, there was a steady growth in the Icelandic economy and money could easily be borrowed at home and abroad. The newly privatized banks grew enormously and many entrepreneurs started businesses all over the world. All went well for a while, but in 2007/8 various crises arose globally and the moneyflow from abroad stopped. The Icelandic banks could not handle the new situation and went bankrupt in October 2008, taking many individuals and enterprises with them in the fall – and almost the Icelandic State itself.

The government tried hard to keep things going with help from the International Monetary Fund. But this huge collapse caused disappointment among ordinary Icelanders, who blamed leading politicians. After demonstrations, the so-called Pots and Pans revolution, the government resigned early in 2009, and the leader of the Social Democratic Alliance, Jóhanna Sigurdardóttir, took over with the Left-Green Movement. These two parties won the election of 2009 and Jóhanna sat on as Prime Minister. That government, in spite of strong opposition, worked like a ”Rubble Rescue Unit“ for the next four years to bring the country's economy back to normal. But many measures that the government was forced to take were not popular, and it lost heavily in the elections of 2013. The two largest parties from that election, the Independence and Progressive Parties, then formed a government with Sigmundur Davíd Gunnlaugsson as Prime Minister.

# Iceland and the World

## The United Nations

Iceland took part in preparations for the establishment of the United Nations towards the end of the war, but was not allowed to be a founding signatory to its charter in autumn 1945. The great powers stipulated that, to qualify for entry, a nation would have to declare war on Germany or Japan or both. The Icelanders refused, maintaining they had done enough for the allied cause by lending their land as a military base during the war. But the world powers of the time would not accept this argument, so Iceland did not join the United Nations until autumn 1946. Since then, it has always been an active member of this remarkable federation of nations and also taken part in the work of many of its special agencies.

## The Keflavík Treaty, 1946

When the Americans took over the defence of Iceland in 1941 and built up military bases in many places around the country, the Icelanders had only consented on the condition that all foreign forces would leave Iceland as soon as the war was over. In the summer of 1945 the war came to an end, but the Americans showed no sign of moving out. In October 1946 the US authorities delivered a message to the Icelandic government with an inquiry about a long-term lease of land for military bases at Keflavík and elsewhere – a period of ninety-nine years was even mentioned. Once this became known, a strong wave of protests broke out against all conveyance of land to the Americans, and they were told that this was quite out of the question. At this time, many Icelanders put their faith in the United Nations as a sufficient force to secure world peace, making such military bases unnecessary. The US put aside its demands, but still stayed in Iceland

Prime minister at this time was Ólafur Thors, who instigated talks with the US on cancelling the treaty of

*The US military base at Keflavík.*

1941 and replacing it with a new one, according to which the Americans promised to remove all their forces from Iceland within a year and a half, and to hand back the Keflavík airfield. Nonetheless, the US military would still be granted free use of the airfield, and permission to station personnel there while they still had forces heavily deployed in Germany. This treaty, to be valid for the following five years, made a rather unfavourable impression and drew widespread protests, especially from the labour unions. But it was finally passed in parliament by thirty-two votes to nineteen.

Once the treaty had come into effect the Socialists, who had voted against it in parliament, walked out of the coalition in protest, bringing the government down. Shortly afterwards, the Americans began to withdraw and had all left within the stipulated time. The country was then free for five years of all military presence, from 1947 to 1951.

### The Marshall Aid, 1948

Most European countries were economically ruined when the World War came to an end in 1945, while the economy of the United States, which had not suf-

172

fered military damage at home, was powerful. The US administration was interested in helping to restore industry among victim countries in Europe, and established a comprehensive aid programme, called the Marshall Aid after the then secretary of state, George Marshall. The Soviet Union would not participate, and then blocked other Eastern European countries from receiving it, ushering in a period of worsening relations between the great powers and the start of the Cold War.

In summer 1948, Iceland signed a five-year treaty under the Marshall Aid programme, thereby obliging itself to take part in the European economic cooperation. When the aid programme ended in 1953, Iceland had received some forty million US dollars, of which it only had to pay back about one quarter. These funds were mainly used to facilitate foreign trade and ease import restrictions, although some were used to support industry and for the construction of hydroelectric power plants, a fertilizer factory and other projects.

In 1950 Iceland joined the European Council in Strasbourg, which promotes European cooperation in cultural affairs and also runs a special court for human rights.

## Membership of NATO, 1949

Soon after the end of World War II in 1945, growing tension between the United States and the Soviet Union developed into the "Cold War". Relations worsened seriously after the communist coup in Czechoslovakia in 1948. To counter growing aggression from the east and possible communist coups in more countries, several western powers under the leadership of the United States prepared a new military alliance against the communist eastern bloc. Iceland, as a non-military nation, would be granted observer status. Initially many Icelanders were against membership of a military alliance, urging a return to the old neutrality. But when it became known that both Denmark and Norway would join NATO, the Icelandic government felt it should follow suit. In March 1949 a delegation from Iceland went to the United States for talks, and returned convinced that it would be a wise move for Iceland to join the new alliance on condition that it did not have to provide armed forces of its own, and that no foreign troops would be stationed in Iceland in peacetime. After some debate, parliament passed a bill for charter membership of the North Atlantic Treaty Organisation on March 30, 1949, by thirty-seven votes to thirteen with two abstentions.

While the treaty was being debated and agreed on March 30, a serious incident took place outside the parliament building. A huge crowd of socialists, labour union members and other opponents had attended open-air meetings earlier in the day and made various resolutions, after which they converged on the parliament building to demand a national referendum on the issue of NATO membership. Aware of the possible demonstrations, leaders of the government parties had broadcast a message asking their supporters to assemble at the Parliament House to prevent trouble or disturbances. The Independence Party had also gathered several hundred volunteers, armed with clubs, for the same purpose.

When it became clear there was a majority in parliament for NATO membership, some demonstrators outside began to throw eggs and stones. Windows were broken and stones rolled on the tables inside. The numerous police and volunteers tried to stop the demonstrators and fighting broke out. After a battle with clubs, stones and all sorts of missiles that caused injuries on both sides, the police fired tear gas to break up the crowd. Soon the square in front of parliament was cleared, but there was extensive damage after the battle. But the rioting resumed that evening with a demonstration at the police station, when the crowd threw stones and broke some windows. The police drove the crowd away with tear gas again and the demonstrations ceased. Iceland had become a member of NATO and on April 4, Bjarni Benediktsson, the minister of foreign affairs, signed the treaty on behalf of Iceland.

The riots on March 30 seem to have been spontaneous and it was never proved that they had been

*Anti-NATO demonstrators rioted outside the parliament building on March 30, 1949.*

planned by socialists, as was sometimes claimed. Most of the demonstrators were simply genuine patriots who did not want their country to be tied to military alliances and operations abroad. A number of people were arrested and imprisoned for their part in the riots, and the incidents and fights of March 30 left scars on daily life in Iceland that took a long time to heal.

### Defence Treaty and Defence Force, 1951

In 1950 the Korean War broke out and international tension rose overnight. The US authorities used the occasion to put pressure on the Icelandic government to allow them to station forces in Iceland in the name of NATO, on the premiss that there was no longer peace in the world. The request arrived during the parliamentary summer recess, but the government of the Independence and Progressive parties called in its members of parliament, and those of the Social Democratic Party, to discuss the request. These parliamentary groups soon agreed on the necessity of allowing some forces to be stationed in the country again, and on May 5, 1951 a defence treaty between Iceland and the United States was signed in accordance with the NATO covenant. Iceland agreed to lend land and

175

other necessary facilities, and in return the United States would take care of the country's military defence. With this new treaty the Keflavík Treaty was revoked and Iceland took over all civil air traffic at Keflavík airport. Regarding possible revocation of the treaty, it was stipulated that either party could ask for a review, and if that still proved inconclusive six months later, the treaty would be annulled twelve months later. Two days after the treaty had been signed the first American soldiers arrived by air at Keflavík, but the treaty was first ratified as law in parliament in the autumn.

Socialist Party members of parliament had not been referred to when the treaty was made and they protested against it, along with various other people. Nevertheless, US forces were to be stationed in Iceland continuously for more than five decades. Throughout this time there was some opposition to the arrangement, with occasional demonstrations. The US administration has never asked for a review of the treaty, but Iceland has done so twice. In 1956 a resolution was passed in parliament to the effect that the troops should leave the country and Iceland itself man all military facilities as a member of NATO. This idea was shelved when the world situation suddenly worsened after the Hungarian uprising and subsequent Warsaw Pact invasion. And in 1971, the newly elected government had decided on a review of the treaty, aiming for a phased withdrawal of all US forces. NATO leaders agitated against the plan, as did groups in Iceland like the Federation for Western Cooperation and a new movement called Defended Land. In the end, the review was made in 1974 by another government, but without any major changes resulting. All this time, there were no serious clashes between Icelanders and the foreign troops, whom the authorities tried to confine within specific boundaries.

Iceland's geographical location in the middle of the Atlantic, along with the Cold War and general air of global tension, combined to maintain the status quo regarding the military presence in Iceland, besides the fact that the Icelanders did not establish any real defence forces of their own. But due to radical chan-

*The Nordic House in Reykjavík.*

ges in world politics in the last few years the military base at Keflavík has lost its former importance. Consequently the Americans slowed down their activities there and after 2000 talks started between the respective governments about changes in the future arrangement. That situation changed suddenly early in 2006 when the American authorities announced that they would withdraw their military forces from Iceland in the fall of that year. By the end of September 2006 they had left and about the same time the Icelandic authorities made a new defence treaty with the Americans.

## The Nordic Council, 1952

Since the people of Iceland have always advocated and promoted as close relations as possible with all the other Nordic nations, it was quite natural for Iceland to join immediately when the Nordic Council was established in 1952. The council holds regular annual meetings, hosted by member nations on a rotating basis, at which representatives from the respective legislative assemblies debate and resolve on common Nordic issues.

Although only a consultative body, the Nordic Council has initiated fruitful cooperation in many areas, including the common Nordic labour market, reciprocal rights to the respective social welfare systems, cooperation among Nordic TV stations, and prizes for literature and musical compositions. On behalf of the

177

Council the Nordic House was built in Reykjavík as a Nordic cultural centre in 1968. A similar institution was established in Tórshavn in the Faroe Islands in 1983 and more such centres are planned elsewhere in the near future.

The Nordic Council has done much to strengthen cultural relations among the Nordic nations and foster the notion of a common Nordic identity.

## Membership of EFTA, 1970

Shortly after peace was established, the countries of Western Europe began increased cooperation in economic affairs and trade. The European economic institution OEEC (later OECD) and Council of Europe were set up in connection with the Marshall Aid programme in 1948, and over the next two decades two free-trade blocs were established, the European Common Market in 1958 that led to the European Economic Community in 1967 (later European Union), and the European Free Trade Association, EFTA, in 1960. There was some debate in Iceland about joining the Common Market, but since this would have forced the nationally vital fishing grounds to be opened up to other nations, the idea was never developed.

Owing to heavy economic dependence on both exports and imports, Iceland has traditionally advocated free international trade, and eventually it was judged to be in the national interest to join EFTA, which was finally done in 1970. Iceland has since concluded trade agreements with the European Union, as other EFTA nations had already done.

Rapid development has been taking place in international trade and commerce over the past few years and, increasingly, EFTA nations have left to join the European Union. At present, Iceland, Norway, Switzerland and Liechtenstein still remain. Protracted negotiations have led to a closer alliance of these two trade blocs with the formation of the European Economic Area of which Iceland is a partner.

*Denmark formally returned the first of the ancient Icelandic manuscripts in 1971.*

## The Manuscripts Returned, 1971

After liberation from the German occupation in 1945, it was quite natural for the King of Denmark and Danes in general to bear a certain amount of resentment towards the Icelanders for having dissolved the union with Denmark while that country suffered under the iron heel of Adolf Hitler during the war. But when peace had been restored, relations between these two, formerly united, countries soon became intimate again.

Much earlier, in the seventeenth century in particular, a large number of ancient Icelandic manuscripts had been sent to Denmark and other Nordic countries. The Icelanders felt, and certainly with a good deal of justification, that these medieval manuscripts belonged to them, and tried to negotiate about them with Denmark. The Danes regarded these antiquities as their lawful possession which it was their duty to take care of as a common Nordic cultural heritage. Negotiations dragged on for years, but in the end an agreement was reached which solved this dispute for good. The majority of the manuscripts were to be given back to Iceland over a specific period, which began when two of the most precious were delivered and presented at a formal ceremony in 1971. The delighted Icelanders built a special archive library in which they keep these priceless national treasures.

*Soviet leader Mikhail Gorbachev and US President Ronald Reagan at the Reykjavík Summmit of 1986*

This noble gesture by the Danes was quite exceptional. Very few, if any, former colonial powers would do or have done anything of the sort. This also shows the good harmony and cooperation which prevail in relations among the Nordic countries. If anything remained at this time of the old hatred towards the Danes among Icelanders, it quickly faded away.

## Tourism – A New Industry

Iceland is no longer an isolated island in the middle of the ocean. Modern communications have put the country in daily contact with the outside world, especially with its closest neighbours on both sides of the Atlantic, and domestic transport and communications have improved enormously. As a consequence, tourism has been a growing industry over the past three or four decades, and over 600,000 foreign visitors now arrive each summer to spend their holidays in the clean air of this country of ice and fire.

And not only regular tourists come to Iceland. In recent years the country has become a popular venue for all kinds of meetings and conferences. Even the leaders of the great powers find it a fitting venue to meet and discuss their problems. For instance, Pompidou and Nixon met there in 1973, and in the autumn of 1986 the superpower leaders from east and west, Gorbachev and Reagan, held their summit meeting in Reykjavík.

# Territorial Waters and Cod Wars

## *Fishery Limit from Three to Four Miles, 1952*

At least since the early fifteenth century fishermen from abroad have travelled to fish in the rich Icelandic waters. In the course of time the foreign fishing effort grew constantly, especially after steam trawlers came into use near the end of the nineteenth century. This fishing from abroad stopped during the two world wars, but when peace had been restored again, the trawlers from Britain, Germany and many other countries returned in great numbers, constantly depleting the most vital resource of the Icelandic people.

The fishery limit was not clearly defined in old times, but from the seventeenth to the nineteenth century it was usually sixteen miles out from the coast. This would not have been unreasonable, had the waters been properly patrolled. But the situation changed suddenly when Denmark made a treaty with the United Kingdom in 1901 about the territorial waters around Iceland, stipulating a fishery limit of only three miles off the coast for the next fifty years. As a result, more fish than ever before were taken, and it soon became clear that the once rich grounds near the coast were being practically ruined by flagrant overfishing. Iceland recognized that action had to be taken, but for a long time was bound by the treaty. The first step was new legislation in 1948 on scientific protection of the fishing grounds around the country. Next was an extension of the limit by one nautical mile off the north coast, and then from three to four nautical miles all around the country in 1952, closing all fjords and bays to trawlers at the same time, which was an important move to protect spawning grounds of cod and other valuable species

All nations, in fact, acknowledged this new limit, except the British. They protested strongly and retaliated by boycotting fish from Iceland for years. Initially this had a bad impact on Icelandic fishermen who were used to selling their fish in British markets. But new markets were found in the United States, the Soviet Union and elsewhere for frozen seafood, so in the long run the boycott was not as harmful as the British may have thought.

### From Four to Twelve Miles, 1958

*Trawl clippers, Iceland's "secret weapon" in the Cod Wars.*

After the middle of the century a major international debate developed about territorial waters and fishery limits. In 1958 the United Nations called an international convention in Geneva on the issue. No common and final agreement was reached, but the majority of nations seemed to favour a twelve-mile limit for coastal states. Determined to wait no longer because of the obvious urgency of protecting stocks, Iceland extended its fishery limit from four to twelve miles on September 1, 1958. On the stipulated day all foreign fishing vessels sailed outside the new limit, except the British. Besides staying inside, they were joined by British naval vessels that prevented the Icelandic coastguard patrol vessels from arresting the British trawlers and taking them to the nearest harbour.

An almost warlike situation developed on the seas around Iceland, which earned the common nickname of the Cod War. Conflicts took various forms, for example when British marines took the crew of a coastguard patrol vessel prisoner to stop one of the British trawlers from being arrested. After keeping the Icelanders on board for some time, they finally gave them a boat and ordered them to row ashore in the middle of the night. This cod war lasted until 1961, when a treaty was finally made in which the British acknowledged the twelve-mile limit, but were granted the right to fish in certain areas between six and twelve miles for the following three years. Also in the treaty was a questionable clause that obliged the Icelanders to seek the sanction of the International Court before extending the limit farther, which caused some difficulties later on.

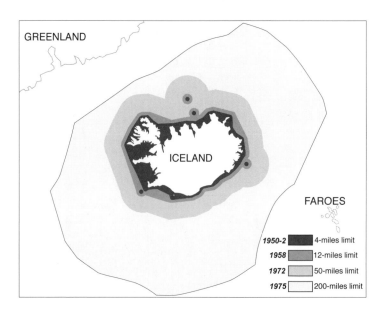

GREENLAND

ICELAND

FAROES

| | |
|---|---|
| **1950-2** | 4-miles limit |
| **1958** | 12-miles limit |
| **1972** | 50-miles limit |
| **1975** | 200-miles limit |

*From Twelve to Fifty Miles, 1972*

*Successive extensions to the fishery limits around Iceland.*

Around 1970, Icelandic politicians began seriously discussing the need to extend the fishery limit even farther, because the grounds were still in obvious need of more protection. The new government that took office in 1971 then decided to extend the limit from twelve to fifty miles the following year. With this action, Iceland had taken the leadership in protection of territorial waters, since most coastal states had stuck to a twelve-mile limit up until that time. Britain and West Germany protested, maintaining that the treaty of 1961 was still in force, which required the sanction of the International Court for further extensions. When Iceland refused to acknowledge the court's right to interfere, the others appealed to it. The court pronounced a preliminary verdict to the effect that British and German trawlers should have the right to fish a certain amount in Icelandic waters. After lodging a protest, Iceland went ahead and declared the new limit.

On September 1, 1972, the fishery limit was extended to fifty miles. Both the British and the Germans refused to acknowledge the new limit and continued

*Lúdvík Jósefsson minister of fisheries during some of the Cod wars.*

to fish inside it. To protect their trawlers from Iceland's coastguard patrol vessels, they brought in reinforced tugboats and other vessels, and confrontations began again. Then the Icelanders produced a "secret weapon": clippers to cut away the trawl nets of offending vessels. Even when the foreign trawlers fished close together with defending vessels all around them, the coastguard crews still proved deft enough with their clippers to foil them. Irritated by constant disturbances, the foreign trawlermen called on their governments for more protection, and in the summer of 1973 the British finally sent frigates to defend their fishing vessels inside Iceland's fifty-mile limit. With the arrival of this naval force a new cod war began, although both sides avoided direct shooting. The British harassed the Icelanders and even rammed coastguard vessels, which were badly damaged but never sunk.

The commanders of the frigates ordered the trawlers to stay in small groups while fishing, so they would be easier to protect, but with little freedom to move, the fishing was invariably poor. In one incident, a skipper lost patience and sailed away to fish on his own, but was spotted by the Icelandic coastguard which fired a couple of shots across his trawler and then one through its hull when he refused to stop. He was on the point of surrender when several British warships arrived and prevented his arrest. Shortly after this, in September 1973, the Icelandic government threatened to recall its ambassador in the UK if the warships were not removed from Icelandic waters. The British yielded and called their frigates back outside the fifty-mile limit. Negotiations began and the Icelandic prime minister went to England for talks with his British colleague, returning with a treaty under which the British promised to withdraw all their warships from Icelandic waters and respect the limit, but were allowed in return a limited catch in several specified areas within the limit over the next two years, although not using large vessels or factory trawlers. The Germans would not negotiate on these terms, so the cod war with them went on. About this time the International Court pronounced its verdict that the extension of the fishery limit around Iceland was unlawful, but Iceland remained undeterred.

## *From Fifty to Two Hundred Miles, 1975*

In 1974 the United Nations called a new international convention in Caracas on the law of the sea, where it soon became obvious that many of the nations supported the principle of a two-hundred-mile jurisdiction for coastal states. Encouraged by this message, Iceland declared that its territorial limit would be extended from fifty to two hundred miles, which the new government formed in autumn 1974 announced would take effect on October 15, 1975.

This final extension duly took effect, at the same time as the 1973 treaty with the British expired. A new cod war ensued, in which the British sent tugboats and warships to protect their trawlers and prevent the Icelandic coastguard from intervening. But about the same time Iceland reached terms with Belgium, West Germany and other nations, whereby they acknowledged the new limit but were allowed limited catches inside it for a stipulated number of years. The British refused to yield, continuing to fish under the protection of warships which rammed the Icelandic coastguard patrol vessels without heeding the damage to their own, much larger vessels. When negotiations broke down, Iceland recalled its ambassador and cut off all

*British frigates attempted in vain to allow fishing within the extended limits.*

diplomatic ties with Great Britain. Despite the intensity of this cod war, the Icelandic coastguard crews refused to be provoked into aggression, and continued to show uncanny skill in avoiding collisions and cutting the nets of British trawlers, which irritated the seamen most of all. It was no wonder that the coastguard captains and crews were regarded, as they had been in 1958 and 1972, almost as national heroes in Iceland.

The increasingly warlike developments on the seas around Iceland were viewed with great anxiety by NATO leaders, who understood the strategic importance of the Keflavík base and feared that Iceland would react by refusing all cooperation with other NATO countries. Intensive work began to find a solution to this dispute and restore peace between these two NATO nations. At the same time, the international climate moved in favour of the Icelandic cause, as more and more countries announced plans to extend their economic jurisdiction to two hundred miles. And finally when the European Community, of which Great Britain was by now a member, decided to extend its own fishery limit and move out to two hundred miles by 1977, the British had no choice but to acknowledge Iceland's own limit and call the cod war to a halt. Negotiations between the two countries began in Oslo, Norway, and on June 1, 1976, a treaty was signed and peace restored again. The UK acknowledged Iceland's two-hundred-mile limit, but was permitted limited fishing rights in certain areas inside its jurisdiction for the next six months. On December 1, 1976, the last British trawler sailed out of Iceland's territorial waters and total victory had been achieved. In the course of a quarter of a century the fishery limit had been extended from three to two hundred miles. Among the many contributing factors, the unflinching action of the coastguard had perhaps played the greatest part, together with the total solidarity on the issue shown by the Icelandic nation. International trends in marine law also helped, and the sympathy and support which Iceland enjoyed as a small country confronting a great power were constantly of great importance.

# Industries and the Environment

## *Agriculture*

The postwar period has seen unparalleled activity in Iceland in which it is fair to say that almost everything has been rebuilt from the foundations. Although sheep and cattle farming has ceased to be the main occupation of most Icelanders, as it was from early times until well into the twentieth century, agriculture is still an important economic activity providing a large number of jobs in production, industry and distribution.

Even as late as 1945, farming in Iceland was still practised along traditional lines, although some technological improvements had been brought about. About half the hay crop was still yielded from grass cut from uncultivated meadows and transported by packhorse for storage. But about mid-century, farming methods were revolutionized by drainage and cultivation of land, greatly increased use of fertilizers, the introduction of motorized vehicles and tractors and all manner of new machinery. At the same time, modern farm houses and other buildings were constructed all over the countryside. With all these improvements production increased rapidly, despite the declining numbers employed in agriculture.

The Farmers' Union was established in 1945 to sa-

*Sheep farming is the mainstay of Icelandic agriculture.*

feguard the economic interests of farmers and regulate agricultural production and prices. Farmers were supposed to enjoy living standards comparable to those of industrial workers and seamen, although in fact they have always been lower. Iceland has now largely stopped export of agricultural products to neighbouring countries, whose own overproduction has led to prohibitively low prices. State subsidies have long been used to keep down prices of agricultural goods for domestic consumption and some export.

Increasing problems in export have meant that agricultural production has been by and large regulated in accordance with domestic demand, and individual farms have been allocated quotas for milk and lamb production since 1980. There are still about 4,000 farmers in Iceland. Most are engaged in sheep and cattle farming, but a growing number live by market gardening, fur farming, poultry, horse breeding, fish farming, tourism, grain growing and forestry.

## Fisheries

Rich waters all around the country, powerful and well-equipped vessels, and above all skilful and hardy seamen contribute to the bumper fish catches which are landed in Iceland every year. But bounteous as they are, Iceland's fishing grounds cannot produce endless harvests, and it has proved necessary to broaden management of offshore stocks by extending the fishery limit in order to conserve the most important resource and basic economic staple of the Icelandic people today.

After World War II the aged fleet was modernized with large-scale purchases of new trawlers and other fishing vessels from abroad, which were distributed among the main fishing harbours around the country with resulting rapid growth in both fishing effort and fisheries production. Cod has always been the most valuable species, although demand is high for other demersal fish as well. Herring, another traditional

*A modern fishing wessel.*

species, has been subject to great catch fluctuations due to overfishing and marine conditions over the years. When the huge spring-spawning stock disappeared in the 1960s it was partly replaced by a smaller pelagic fish, capelin, which has been taken in huge quantities since, largely for meal and oil production. Catches of a different, local herring stock have been increasing in recent years.

About 1970, the fishing fleet had become obsolete once more, and was duly renewed with modern trawlers, both imported and domestic-built. For many years the fleet continued to grow until eventually it was far too powerful and productive for the catch that could safely be taken. A smaller cod catch diverted fishing towards a number of other species, but they were also limited. Eventually, to curb the fishing effort, a system of quotas for both vessels and species was introduced in 1984, which has been in force ever since.

Fishing, fish processing and all kinds of related industries are the basic industry and livelihood of most towns and villages all over the country. Conservation and sensible utilization of valuable marine resources through controls such as quotas are therefore vital to prevent irreparable damage to the very foundation of the nation's economy.

Many foreign nations practised whaling in Icelandic waters over the centuries. In the late nineteenth and early twentieth centuries whaling off Iceland was largely in the hands of Norwegians, who operated a number of whaling stations in both the east and west of the country. After stocks became seriously depleted, all whaling off Iceland was prohibited in 1915 for conservation reasons, and only begun again, by Icelanders, from a single station in 1948. Iceland undertook small-scale whaling and halted commercial catches under an international Whaling Commission moratorium that took effect in 1986.

## Energy, Industry and Service

Although Iceland completely lacks many natural resources such as minerals, oil and coal, it is all the richer in energy contained in numerous rivers and hot springs all over the country. Natural hot water from geothermal springs now provides space heating and hot tap water for much of the country. A heating system of this type was established for the city of Reykjavík in 1945 and this pollution-free energy source is now exploited where available all over the country, providing heating for more than 90% of all Icelandic homes. In recent years geothermal energy has also been used to produce electricity, while geothermal hot water has been utilized to heat greenhouses for growing vegetables and even fruit since its introduction for this purpose in 1923.

Shortly after World War II two new power plants were built on the river Sog, and the power station on the river Laxá in the north was enlarged. Although

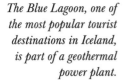

*The Blue Lagoon, one of the most popular tourist destinations in Iceland, is part of a geothermal power plant.*

this sufficed to meet demand at the time, the situation changed when ideas arose around 1960 for encouraging foreign investment in power-intensive industries. Negotiations were begun with the multinational Swiss Aluminium, which could only be realized with a massive increase in electricity production. A new power plant was then built on the Thjórsá river at Mount Búrfell in south central Iceland. Formally opened in 1970, Búrfell is the largest plant in the country, with a capacity of around 270 megawatts. A few years later two similar plants were built close by and more new power stations are under construction or planned.

A number of power-intensive ventures use energy from hydro- and geothermal power stations, including an aluminium smelter near Hafnarfjördur, which has been in operation since 1969, a ferrosilicon smelter at Grundartangi in Hvalfjördur, which opened in 1979, and a new aluminium smelter also in Hvalfjördur, which opened in 1998. At present a further aluminium smelter is under construction in Reydarfjördur in east Iceland in connection with a huge new power plant which is being built in the eastern highlands. There has also been a fertilizer plant near Reykjavík since 1954, a cement works at Akranes since 1958 and the diatomite drying plant at Lake Mývatn, which was operational from 1966 to 2005 and used mainly electricity generated by geothermal steam.

Although these new industries have provided a large amount of employment, more people work elsewhere in sectors such as fish processing, the wool and skin industries, construction, shipbuilding, various types of food production and a wide range of skilled and unskilled manufacturing. There has been a marked growth in the commerce, banking, public and private clerical sectors and other services in general.

Most of the numerous local and job-specific labour unions belong to a national federation, and the employers have their own counterpart confederation. Governmental and municipal officials belong to a separate federation, while university graduate civil servants have their own union. Strikes and industrial disputes in pursuit of pay claims have been fairly common and a special government official, the State Arbitrator, mediates in such instances.

## Communications

Automobiles and aircraft are now the most common means of communication in Iceland. Shipping is nonetheless very useful and of vital importance for the export and import trade. Passenger sea transport is minimal except by the few regular ferry services. During the war, airports were built at Reykjavík and Keflavík and others have since been built at Akureyri, Ísafjördur, Egilsstadir, Höfn, the Westman Islands, Saudárkrókur and Húsavík, along with smaller airfields at a number of other places.

Automobile ownership has mushroomed in the past four or five decades and there are now more than 150,000 private cars among a population of less than 300,000, besides a great number of lorries, buses and other kinds of vehicles. At the same time, a relatively effective road system has been developed around the country. The Ring Road looping Iceland was completed in 1974, after roads and bridges had been built that overcome the problem of flooding on the sandy stretches in the southeast. New bridges have been built in many other places, for instance across the fjord at Borgarnes in 1980. Several tunnels have been dug through difficult cliffs and mountains, for instance near Siglufjördur and Ólafsfjördur in the north, and in the west and east of Iceland. A very important tunnel which links Reykjavík and Akranes was dug under the Hvalfjördur fjord and opened in 1998. Gravel roads are still common outside built-up areas, but every year more and more roads are asphalted.

Flying has become a very common means of transport and scheduled services now link Iceland with a number of cities on both sides of the Atlantic every day. Frequent domestic air services also link all major areas of the country; it has been said that in a way the Icelanders jumped straight from horseback to the aeroplane. Two airlines handled the bulk of international air services from 1945 until 1973, when they merged. A few other airlines also operate, both for international and domestic traffic.

Construction of airfields, harbours, roads and bridges is continually under way, since good communications are of vital importance in modern Iceland. But since the country is sparsely populated, mountainous and rugged, such work looks set to continue for the foreseeable future.

## Nature and Environment

Iceland's vegetation is inherently delicate and has been impaired or destroyed in various ways ever since human habitation began in the country. The worst loss was with the virtual destruction of the old birch forests in the course of time, since that left the soil too dry and prone to erosion by wind and water, heat and cold. Soil erosion is one of the biggest problems facing the Icelandic people. Since the beginning of the last century much has been done to halt erosion and cultivate new vegetation in various places. A large number of individuals and societies are engaged in "reclothing the land", along with two governmental institutions engaged in soil conservation, land reclamation and afforestation, which certainly give some hope that the trend will eventually be reversed in the future.

Well into the last century, little attention was paid to nature and the environment as such, but a change for the better has taken place in the past few decades. About 1970 there was a plan to flood a fine valley in the north to create a huge reservoir for a hydroelectric power plant. Local people were vocal in their opposition to the scheme, and although they were not much listened to in the beginning, public opinion began to change after years of protests. Eventually, the value of protecting nature was seen to outweigh the value of a reservoir in the valley, and the plan was abandoned. If the situation had arisen a few decades earlier, probably nobody would have said or done anything to stop it. Among the results of growing interest in the protection of nature has been the establishment of a number of national parks and reserves. A significant step forward

*The town in Westman Islands was temporarily evacuated when a volcanic eruption began on its outskirts in 1973.*

was also taken in 1990 when a ministry of the environment was finally set up.

By the same token, the Icelandic environment itself is often dangerous to man, with widespread risk of various kinds of natural calamity, such as floods and storms, avalanches, volcanic eruptions and earthquakes. The country is still being formed, as shown by the submarine eruption of 1963, when a new island was born out of the sea overnight, southwest of the Westman Islands. In 1973 one of the biggest eruptions in modern times began on the outskirts of the only town on the Westman Islands. All 5,000 inhabitants had to be evacuated immediately and most of the town was buried under lava and ash. When the eruption stopped several months later, the inhabitants returned, setting to work to clean up the town and build new houses to replace those lost. Such events are inherent in the volatile world of nature that the Icelanders have to live with. They have grown used to it and, we might say, become a part of it.

# Cultural Trends and National Life

## Schools and Education

A new education act of 1974 made nine years' schooling compulsory for all children, from seven to sixteen, which remained the case until 1990 when it was increased by a year, with children starting at the age of six. Teacher training has been reformed in many ways and in 1972 the old Teachers' College in Reykjavík was authorized to teach at university level. When the Republic was proclaimed in 1944 there were only two secondary grammar schools in the country, in Reykjavík and Akureyri. Now there are a number of secondary grammar and comprehensive schools all over the country, which award a matriculation certificate granting the right to university entrance, besides a variety of vocational colleges. New legislation for secondary education was introduced in 1988.

The University of Iceland has grown very rapidly with the addition of many new faculties, and the number of students attending it has increased accordingly, even though it is still fairly common to study overseas. For a long time this university was the only tertiary academic institution in the country, but new schools and academic institutions have come into existence in the last few years, such as the Teacher Training College in Reykjavík, the Agricultural Colleges at Hvanneyri and Hólar, the Technical College and University College in Reykjavík, which have now merged, the

*The main building of the University of Iceland.*

195

University of Akureyri, founded in 1987, the Business College at Bifröst and the brand-new Icelandic Academy of the Arts in Reykjavík, founded in 1999. A fairly wide range of scientific research is conducted at the universities as well as at specialized research institutes.

## Church and Religion

*Hallgrímskirkja Church in Reykjavík.*

The Icelandic State Lutheran Church has held its ground for the most part and adapted to changing outlooks and lifestyles. Religious controversy reigned for some decades early in the twentieth century between old and new theology, or conservative and liberal views in religious matters, and a few free churches were established in that period. Spiritualism and sectarian trends also kindled disputes, and a number of new sects have taken root. A Catholic mission has been working in the country since about 1860, and established schools and hospitals which it still runs. A Catholic bishop has been installed in Reykjavík and a few Catholic congregations have developed.

Nonetheless, the Lutheran State Church easily remains predominant in the religious life of the Icelanders, and about 76% of the population nominally belongs to it. Since 1801 the Icelandic Church has been led by one bishop in Reykjavík, although two suffragan bishops have served since 1909, one in the north and the other in the south. The Church is the second-oldest institution of the Icelandic people; only the legislative assembly, the Althing, is older. Christianity was introduced in AD1000 and a large festival was held for the millennial celebration of the Church and Christianity in Iceland in 2000.

## Literature and the Arts

*Writer Ólafur Jóhann Sigurdsson.*

Under the Republic, life in Iceland has undergone far more radical changes than ever before in the history of the nation. In literature and the arts, these radical changes have been clearly reflected in drastic revolts against earlier concepts of form and structure in po-

*Poet Snorri Hjartarson.*

*Writer
Thor Vilhjálmsson.*

*Writer
Frida Á. Sigurdardóttir.*

etry, painting, sculpture and elsewhere. Within a very short period of time, Iceland saw a world war begin and end and was occupied by foreign forces, cut the last ties that bound it to a foreign country and established its own free and independent republic. Shortly afterwards came the Cold War, membership of NATO, the military base at Keflavík and the long presence of US forces on Icelandic soil. These were all controversial signs of the times which caused deep divisions among the Icelandic people, and countless other developments stirred up the old and once timeless society, such as new industries, technological revolutions, huge migration from the countryside into towns and villages, industrial strife and strikes, nationalism and internationalism, together with ever-increasing contact with the outside world. Icelandic life had become virtually unrecognizable, and the soul of the nation strove to come to terms with this new state of affairs, both in day-to-day living and in creative work.

From the legions of new literary figures who emerged after the war, the leading names alone make a long list: poets like Snorri Hjartarson (1906–1986), Jón Jónsson (1917–2000), Stefán Hördur Grímsson (1919–2002), Einar Bragi (1921–2005), Jónas Svafár (b 1925–2004), Hannes Sigfússon (1922–1997), Jón Óskar (1927–1998), Sigurdur A Magnússon (b.1928), Hannes Pétursson (b 1931), Matthías Johannessen (b 1930) and Jóhann Hjálmarsson (b 1939); and novelists such as Halldór Laxness (1902–1998), Ólafur Jóhann Sigurdsson (1918–1988), Elías Mar (b 1924–2007), Indridi G Thorsteinsson (1926–2000), Jóhannes Helgi (1926–2001), Thor Vilhjálmsson (b 1925–2011), Ingimar Erlendur Sigurdsson (b 1933 ), Jakobína Sigurdardóttir (1918–1995), Svava Jakobsdóttir (1930–2004), Thorgeir Thorgeirson (1933 –2005), Gudbergur Bergsson (b 1932) and Frída Sigurdardóttir (b 1940–2010).

Halldór Laxness, who began writing while still in his teens and was most productive in the 1930s, is by far the best-known Icelandic author in our time and has done more than any other writer to establish Iceland in the literary world, with a career crowned by becoming the only Icelandic Nobel Prize-winner in 1955. Several Icelandic poets and novelists have won the

*Writer*
*Einar Már Gudmundsson.*

*Writer Sjón*
*(Sigurjón B. Sigurdson).*

*Composer*
*Björk Gudmundsdóttir.*

Nordic Council Prize for Literature: Snorri Hjartarson, Ólafur Jóhann Sigurdsson, Thor Vilhjálmsson, Frída Sigurdardóttir, Einar Már Gudmundsson, Sjón (Sigurjón B Sigurdsson) and Gyrdir Elíasson The Council's companion prize for composers has been won by Atli Heimir Sveinsson, Haflidi Hallgrímsson, Björk Gudmundsdóttir and Haukur Tómasson.

Literature is not the only branch of the arts which is flourishing; painting, sculpture, music, theatre and film are all dynamic and well represented. State radio services began in 1930 and state television in 1966, and with increased freedom in this field since 1986 a number of commercial radio stations and commercial TV stations have come into being. But this massive output of mass media largely seems to have taken place without dampening public interest in the written word through newspapers, magazines and books.

## Sports and Games

Interest and participation in sports of all kinds run very high in Iceland, especially among young people. Soccer, handball and similar sports are practised in large numbers, and gymnastic halls, swimming pools and athletics tracks are found all over the country. At an international level, some Icelanders have become European champions in their sport and three have won Olympic medals. A number of Icelanders play for leading soccer teams abroad, and in other professional sports.

Chess has long been a tradition in Iceland and an exceptional proportion of the population are active chess players. Many chess players have established themselves on the international tournament circuit and Iceland is said to have more grandmasters and international masters per capita of population than any other nation. Perhaps Iceland's greatest chess honour, however, was when the world championship match between Boris Spassky and Robert Fischer was held in Reykjavík in 1972, which proved to be a very stimulating event for national interest in chess.

Bridge is another popular and growing sport, boos-

*Writer*
*Gyrðir Elíasson.*

ted by a sudden wave of mass interest when Iceland won the world championship in 1991.

## Equal Rights

The women's rights movement which began in the nineteenth century has continued with varying intensity ever since. A long campaign to win equal pay for the same work led to a law to this effect in 1957. Legislation about holiday allowance payments for housewives was passed in 1960 and a law from 1971 established equal social security rights for both men and women. The same age of consent for both sexes, 18 years, was made law in 1972.

Around 1970 the feminist ("Red Stocking") movement reached Iceland. In 1970 a woman politician became a government minister for the first time, and in 1974 the first female member of the clergy was ordained. During the international women's

Year, 1975, women in Iceland staged a mass strike from work both at home and outside on October 24, which has been repeated at intervals several times since then. Legislation on abortion, equal taxation and other issues has been enacted more recently.

But although women won a large number of their demands, many agreed that the best way towards direct political influence was through a female-only election candidature. This was launched in the 1982 municipal elections, when feminists won city council seats in both Reykjavík and Akureyri. A similar platform, the Women's Alliance, contested the parliamentary election in 1983, and won three seats in the Althing. At the next general election in 1987, the Women's Alliance increased its representation to six seats, but slipped to five in 1991 and still fewer in 1995. In the 1999 parliamentary election the Women's Alliance formed an alliance with two other leftist parties and this became the Coalition Party in 2000. Although the Women's Alliance was never involved in government, its members said that parliamentary representation itself, and the accompanying influence on legislation

*Mass demonstration in the centre of Reykjavík to mark the "women's strike" of Oktober 24, 1975.*

and the political debate, served the cause of equal rights in general in the long run.

Growing public awareness of equal rights issues has been especially clear in support for the cause of the disabled, which has been promoted by a variety of legislation including a specific act of parliament in 1979, and an elaboration upon it in 1983.

### The Festival of the Settlement, 1974

In 1974, according to historical tradition, eleven centuries had passed since the settlement of Iceland began. The occasion was marked that summer by celebrations all over the country, including a grand national festival at Thingvellir on July 29, where about 60,000 people gathered. It began with a normal meeting of the Althing, held on this occasion on the site of the old parliament, at which members of parliament passed a resolution on greatly increased financial support for soil reclamation and afforestation work. It was followed by a programme of traditional song and music, speeches by the president and the prime minister, readings by poets and writers and performances of many kinds. Also attended by a number of foreign delegates and representatives who brought congratulations and gifts from their nations to the Icelandic people, this was the largest gathering that has ever been held in the country.

The anniversary was also marked by various other commemorative events and milestones, perhaps the most noteworthy being the completion of roads and bridges across the flood-prone sands of the southeast, which thereby allowed the Ring Road to be opened around the entire country.

## Lifestyles

In the course of some half a century Iceland has changed from a poor, undeveloped and mostly rural society into a largely urban one which ranks with the most developed and progressive countries in the world. Educational and schooling systems, public health and social security are among the best in the developed world. All Icelanders have the means to meet their basic, everyday needs and unemployment is virtually unknown. Lifestyles have changed accordingly, and higher demands are made in standards of living than ever before. Housing has to be bigger, lavishly furnished and equipped with all modern conveniences. Private cars are no longer a luxury but a common necessity for most homes. People eat more varied and better food, and have more time for the ever-growing range of leisure and entertainment that is available. Travelling, in Iceland and abroad, is quite natural for most people.

But the new lifestyle has been won at a price. A long

*Kárahnjúkar power plant in East Iceland under construction.*

working day is the norm for most people and it has become customary for both men and women to go out to work. The structure and nature of the home and family have changed as a result, and children are brought up for much of the time in nurseries and schools. Old people, too, have lost their traditional place in the home, and most of them spend their last years in official care. For better or worse, this development has been going on for several decades. Constant demands for higher living standards hit children and old people worst, but also affect the people who themselves take part in the race for an even better lifestyle. It may be said that this is characteristic not only of a great number of individuals, but also of Icelandic society in general, where domestic and foreign debts cast long shadows into the future.

## New Age of Settlement

The population of Iceland has grown very fast since the beginning of the twentieth century. In 1901 Iceland had 78,470 inhabitants, in 1950 they numbered 143,973 and in 2001 the number had become 286,575 and reached 300,000 in 2006. A hundred years ago

Iceland was largely a rural society, but after radical changes the great majority of the population now live in towns and villages. Reykjavík, the capital, is by far the biggest town with about 115,000 inhabitants, and in the Greater Reykjavík area the number is about 185,000.

From the beginning of the twentieth century and most of all since about 1940, people have been moving at an accelerating rate from the countryside into more densely populated areas. A new age of settlement has been going on. In medieval times came the first age of settlement, when immigrants came from abroad, spread all over the country and settled down. But in this modern age of settlement the trend is reversed: people are moving from the countryside where their roots lie far back in time, to make new settlements in towns and villages with the aim of leading a better life and building up a new kind of society.

The Icelandic people lived very much in the same way from the time their history began in the Middle Ages, right down to the last century. But everything has changed, and the Icelanders have made colossal advances in a very short time: they are now just as modern and socially and technologically developed as their neighbours to the east and west. In the turmoil of new and changing times, countless old customs and values are inevitably lost. In light of that fact, it is still quite remarkable how well this young nation has preserved its language and identity, the same ancient culture and heritage which inspired it in the first place to re-assert itself in the modern age.

*Restaurant Perla in Reykjavík.*

# Bibliography

Aðalgeir Kristjánsson: Brynjólfur Pétursson. 1972.

Annálar 1400-1800 I-V. Rvík 1922-59.

Arnór Sigurjónsson: Frá árdögum ísl. þjóðar. Rvík 1973.

Aschehougs Verdenshistorie I-VIII. Oslo 1953-58.

Barði Guðmundsson: Uppruni Íslendinga. Rvík 1959.

Bergsteinn Jónsson: Tryggvi Gunnarsson III. Rvík 1972.

Biskupasögur Sögufélagsins I-II. Rvík 1903-15.

Bjarni Benediktsson: Land og lýðveldi I-II. Rvík 1965-75.

Björn Þorsteinsson: Íslenka þjóðveldið. Rvík 1953.

Björn Þorsteinsson: Íslenska skattlandið. Rvík 1956.

Björn Þorsteinsson: Enska öldin. Rvík 1970.

Björn Þorsteinsson: Tíu þorskastríð. Rvík 1976.

Brynleifur Tóbíasson: Þjóðhátíðin 1874. Rvík 1958.

Danmarks historie I-X. Kbh. 1962.

Egill Stardal: Jón Loftsson. Rvík 1967.

Einar Laxness: Íslandssaga I-III. Rvík 1995.

Eggert Ólafsson & Bjarni Pálsson: Ferðabók I-II. Rvík 1943.

Garrett & Godfrey: Europe since 1815. New York 1947.

Gils Guðmundsson: Skútuöldin I-II. Rvík 1955-56.

Gils Guðmundsson: Öldin sem leið I-II. Rvík1950-51.

Gils Guðmundsson: Öldin okkar I-II. Rvík 1950-51.

Grimbergs Verdenshistorie I-XVII. Kbh. 1970.

Guðjón Friðriksson: Ég elska þig stormur. Rvík 2005.

Gunnar Benediktsson: Snorri skáld í Reykholti. Rvík 1957.

Gunnar Karlsson: Frá endurskoðun til valtýsku. Rvík 1972.

Haraldur Matthíasson: Landið og Landnáma I-II. Rvík 1983.

Heimir Pálsson: Straumar og stefnur. Rvík 1978.

Heimir Þorleifsson: Frá einveldi til lýðveldis. Rvík 1983.

Helgi P. Bríem: Sjálfstæði Íslands 1809. Rvík 1936.

Holmsen & Jensen: Norges historie I-II. Oslo 1949.

Indriði G. Þorsteinsson: Þjóðhátíðin 1974. Rvík 1986.

Íslenskt fornbréfasafn I-XVI. Kbh. & Rvík 1857-1972.

Íslensk fornrit I-XXVIII. Rvík 1933-68.

Jarðabók Árna Magnússonar og Páls Vídalín I-XI. Kbh. 1913-43.

Jón J. Aðils: Einokunarverslun Dana á Íslandi. Rvík 1919.

Jón J. Aðils: Gullöld Íslendinga. Rvík 1948.

Jón Guðnason: Skúli Thoroddsen I-II. Rvík1968-74.

Jón Helgason: Öldin átjánda I-II. Rvík 1960-61.

Jón Helgason: Öldin sautjánda. Rvík 1966.

Jón R. Hjálmarsson: Brautryðjendur. Skógum 1973.

Jón Jóhannesson: Íslendingasaga I-II. Rvík 1956-58.

Jón Steingrímsson: Ævisaga. Rvík 1945.

Jón Þ. Þór: Dr. Valtýr. Ak. 2004.

Jónas Jónasson: Íslenskir þjóðhættir. Rvík 1945.

Kristján Albertsson: Hannes Hafstein I-III. Rvík 1961-85.

Kristján Eldjárn: Kuml og haugfé. Rvík 1956.

Lúðvík Kristjánsson: Íslenskir sjávarhættir. Rvík 1980.

Lýður Björnsson: Skúli fógeti. Rvík 1966.

Lýðveldishátíðin 1944. Rvík 1945.

Magnús Jónsson: Saga Íslendinga IX. Rvík 1957.

Merkir Íslendingar I-VII. Rvík 1947-57.

Ólafur Briem: Heiðinn siður á Íslandi. Rvík 1945.
Ólafur R. Einarsson: Frá landnámi til Lúterstrúar. Rvík 1980.
Ólafur Hansson: Gissur jarl. Rvík 1966.
Páll E. Ólason et al.: Íslenskar æviskrár. Rvík 1948-76.
Páll E. Ólason: Saga Íslendinga IV-V. Rvík 1942-44.
Páll E. Ólason & Þorkell Jóhannesson: Saga Íslendinga VI.
    Rvík 1946.
Saga Íslands. Ritstj. Sigurður Líndal. I-VII. Rvík 1974-94.
Schevill, Ferdinant: A History of Europe. New York 1950.
Sigurður Nordal: Íslensk menning. Rvík 1946.
Sigurður Þórarinsson: The Thousand Years' Struggle Against Ice
    and Fire. Rvík 1956.
Snorri Sturluson: Heimskringla. Rvík 1944.
Sveinn Björnsson: Endurminningar. Rvík 1957.
Sveinn Pálsson: Ferðabók. Rvík 1945.
Sverrir Kristjánsson: Ræður og riss. Rvík 1962.
Taviani, Paolo Emilio: Columbus, The Great Adventure.
    New York 1991.
Þorkell Jóhannesson: Saga Íslendinga VII. Rvík 1962.
Þór Whitehead: Ófriður í aðsigi. Rvík1982.
Þór Whitehead: Milli vonar og ótta. Rvík 1995.
Þórhallur Guttormsson: Jón biskup Arason. Rvík 1968.

# Index

Alberti 123
Albrecht of Mecklenburg 62
Ari Jónsson 74
Ari Thorgilsson 10, 42, 43
Arngrímur Jónsson 83
Atli Heimir Sveinsson 198
Audur the Deep-minded 17
Árni Páll Árnason 166
Árni Magnússon 84, 85
Árni Oddsson 80
Árni Thorláksson 60
Ásgeir Ásgeirsson 149, 162, 163
Ásgrímur Jónsson 153
Ásmundur Sveinsson 42, 153

Balbo 146
Baldvin Einarsson 102, 103
Bede, the Venerable 10
Benedikt Gröndal (politician) 165, 166, 168
Benedikt Gröndal (poet) 113
Benedikt Jónsson Gröndal 96
Benedikt Sveinsson 122
Bergur Thorberg 110
Bernadotte, Jean-Baptiste/ Karl Johan 100
Bismarck 108
Bjarni Benediktsson (Prime Minister) 164, 165, 168, 174
Bjarni Benediktsson (current leader of the Independence Party) 164
Bjarni Herjólfsson 26
Bjarni Pálsson 87
Bjarni Saemundsson 129
Bjarni Thorarensen 101
Bjarni Thorsteinsson 153
Björk Gudmundsdóttir 198
Björn Gunnlaugsson 113
Björn Halldórsson 90
Björn Jónsson (priest) 74
Björn Jónsson (editor) 122, 135
Björn Jónsson (historian) 83
Björn M Olsen 130
Björn Thórdarson 150, 159
Björn Thorleifsson 65
Bríet Bjarnhédinsdóttir 132
Brynjólfur Bjarnason 150
Brynjólfur Pétursson 103

Brynjólfur Sveinsson 80, 83

Charles V 68
Christensen, I C 134
Christian Frederick/Christian VIII 100, 104, 105
Christian II 68
Christian III 68
Christian IX 108, 114, 115, 133
Christian X 137, 151, 160
Columbus 27, 28
Craxton, John Williamson 65

Dadi Gudmundsson 73
Davíd Oddsson 168
Davíd Stefánsson 153
Diciulus 10
Dietrich of Minden 71

Eggert Ólafsson 87
Egill Skallagrímsson 23
Einar Arnórsson 138
Einar Benediktsson 122, 123, 124, 133
Einar Már Gudmundsson 198
Einar Jónsson 153
Einar H Kvaran 122
Einar Olgeirsson 150, 151, 165
Einar Sigurdsson 83
Einar Bragi Sigurdsson 197
Eiríkur Thorvaldsson/ Eric the Red 25
Elías Mar 197
Emil Jónsson 165, 168
Eric of Pommern 62, 65, 66
Eysteinn Jónsson 165

Finnur Jónsson (bishop) 96
Finnur Jónsson (linguist) 130
Finnur Jónsson (painter) 153
Fischer, Robert 198
Flóki Vilgerdarson/Raven-Flóki 13, 14
Frederick II 68
Frederick III 80
Frederick IV 85
Frederick VI 103
Frederick VII 105
Frederick VIII 133, 137
Fridbjörn Steinsson 130

Friedrich (missionary) 29
Frída Sigurdardóttir 197, 198

Gardar Svavarsson 12, 13
Geir H Haarde 164, 169
Geir Hallgrímsson 164, 166, 168
Gestur Pálsson 121, 131
Gissur Einarsson 71, 72
Gissur Ísleifsson 37–40, 43
Gissur Thorvaldsson 52–55, 58, 58
Gissur the White 30, 36
Gísli Brynjólfsson 113
Gísli Magnússon the Wise 83
Gísli Sveinsson 160
Gorbachev 180
Gregory VII 38
Grímur Geitskör 21
Grímur Thomsen 113
Gudbergur Bergsson 197
Gudbrandur Thorlákssson 81, 82, 83
Gudmundur Arason 48, 49
Gudmundur Bödvarsson 153
Gudmundur Daníelsson 153
Gudmundur Fridjónsson 122
Gudmundur G Hagalín 153
Gudmundur Kamban 153
Gudni Ágústsson 165
Gudrídur Thorbjarnardóttir 27
Gunnar Gunnarsson 153
Gunnar Thoroddsen 167, 168
Gunnbjörn Úlfsson 25
Gustav Ericson Vasa 62, 68
Gylfi Th Gíslason 165
Gyrdir Elíasson 198

Haflidi Hallgrímsson 198
Halldór Ásgrímsson 165, 168, 169
Halldór Laxness 153, 154, 197
Hallgrímur Pétursson 83
Hallveig Fródadóttir 16
Hannes Finnsson 95, 96
Hannes Hafstein 122–128, 134–138
Hannes Pétursson 197
Hannes Sigfússon 197
Hannes Thorsteinsson 135

Hannibal Valdemarsson 165, 167
Haraldur Bluetooth 34
Haraldur Fairhair 17, 34
Haraldur Gudmundsson 165
Harboe, Ludvig 86
Haukur Tómasson 198
Hákon Hákonarson 51, 57, 207
Hákon VI 62
Hédinn Valdemarsson 150, 151
Helga, sister of Ingólfur 15
Helga Sigurdardóttir 74
Helgi the Lean 17
Henry III 36
Henry IV 38
Henry VIII 68
Hermann Jónasson 149, 150, 155, 165, 167
Hilmar Finsen 108, 109, 110
Hitler, Adolf 151, 154, 179
Hjalti Skeggjason 30
Hjálmar Jónsson 113
Hjörleifur Hródmarsson 14, 15
Hrollaugur Rögnvaldsson 17

Indridi G Thorsteinsson 197
Ingibjörg H Bjarnason 132
Ingibjörg Einarsdóttir 119
Ingibjörg Sólrún Gísladóttir 164, 166
Ingimar Erlendur Sigurdsson 197
Ingimundur the Old 17
Ingólfur Arnarson 14–17, 20, 91, 114
Ísleifur Gissurarson 36, 37, 42

Jakobína Sigurdardóttir 197
Jones, Alexander 99
Jóhann Hafstein 164, 165, 168
Jóhann Hjálmarsson 197
Jóhann Sigurjónsson 153
Jóhanna Sigurdardóttir 166, 169, 170
Jóhannes Helgi 197
Jóhannes Jónasson 153
Jóhannes S Kjarval 153
Jón Arason 69–75, 81
Jón Árnason 113
Jón Baldvinsson 132
Jón Eiríksson 95
Jón Espólín 101

Jón Gerreksson 65
Jón Baldvin Hannibalsson 165
Jón Jónsson 197
Jón Leifs 153
Jón Magnússon 138, 140, 141, 147, 148
Jón Ólafsson 122
Jón Óskar 197
Jón Sigurdsson 107, 108, 110, 118, 119, 122, 129, 142
Jón Sigurdsson from Gautlönd 122
Jón Sigurdsson (party leader) 165
Jón Stefánsson 153
Jón Steingrímsson 94
Jón Sveinsson/Nonni 153
Jón Thorkelsson 86
Jón Thorkelsson Vídalín 84
Jón Thorláksson (poet) 96
Jón Thorláksson (politician) 148
Jón Thoroddsen 113
Jón Trausti/ Gudmundur Magnússon 122
Jón Ögmundsson 39, 40, 43, 48
Jónas Hallgrímsson 103
Jónas Jónasson 121
Jónas Jónsson 132, 148, 149
Jónas Svafár 197
Jörgensen, Jörgen 98, 99

Karl Jónsson 57
Katrín Jakobsdóttir 166
Ketilbjörn the Old 17
Ketill Thorsteinsson 43
Kjartan Jóhannsson 165
Klaus von Mervitz 71
Kolbeinn Arnórsson 52, 53
Konrád Gíslason 103
Kristján Eldjárn 162, 163
Kristján Jónsson (poet) 113
Kristján Jónsson (politician) 135, 136
Kristmann Gudmundsson 153

Leifur Eiríksson/ Leif Ericson 26
Lindbergh, Charles 146
Luther, Martin 68
Lúdvík Jósepsson 165, 184

Magnús Grímsson 113
Magnús the Reformer 57, 59

Magnús Stephensen (judge) 96, 101
Magnús Stephensen (governor) 110
Marconi 128
Margaret, daughter of King Valdemar 62
Margrét Frímannsdóttir 165
Marshall, George 173
Marteinn Einarsson 72
Matthías Jochumsson 112, 113
Matthías Johannessen 197
Milton 96

Naddoddur 12
Napoleon 97, 100
Náttfari 12, 13
Nelson 146
Nixon 180

Oddur Einarsson 82
Oddur Gottskálksson 69
Oluf Hákonarson 62

Ólafur Briem 132
Ólafur Fridriksson 131
Ólafur Ragnar Grímsson 163, 165
Ólafur Haraldsson 31, 33, 35
Ólafur Jóhannesson 165, 166, 168
Ólafur Ólafsson/Olavius 88
Ólafur Jóhann Sigurdsson 196, 197, 198
Ólafur Stephensen 96
Ólafur Thors 148, 150, 164, 166, 167, 168, 171
Ólafur Tryggvason 29, 34
Ólöf Loftsdóttir 65

Páll Briem 123
Páll Vídalín 85
Pompidou 180
Pytheas 9

Rafn, Carl Christian 101
Ragnar Arnalds 165
Rask, Rasmus Christian 101
Reagan 180
Rudolf 36
Runólfur Thorláksson 43

Saemundur Sigfússon the Wise 42

Sigfús Eymundsson 114
Sighvatur Björgvinsson 165
Sigmundur Davíd Gunn-
laugsson 165, 169, 170
Sigurdur Eggerz 138, 142, 147
Sigurdur Gudmundsson 113,
114
Sigurdur A Magnússon 197
Sigurdur Pétursson 96 208
Sigurjón B Sigurdsson/Sjón
198
Skafti Thóroddsson 36
Skallagrímur Kveldúlfsson 17
Skúli Bárdarson 51, 52
Skúli Magnússon 89–92, 95
Skúli Thoroddsen 134, 135
Smidur Andrésson 61
Snaebjörn Galti 25
Snorri Hjartarson 197, 198
Snorri Sturluson 50, 51, 52,
57, 58
Snorri Thorfinnsson 27
Spassky, Boris 198
Stefán Hördur Grímsson 197
Stefán Ólafsson 83
Stefán Sigurdsson 153
Stefán Stefánsson 129
Stefán Jóhann Stefánsson 164,
165, 166
Stefán Stephensen 99
Stefnir Thorgilsson 29
Stephan G Stephansson 121
Steingrímur Hermannsson
165, 167, 169

Steingrímur J Sigfússon 166
Steingrímur Steinthórsson 167
Steingrímur Thorsteinsson
113
Steinn Steinarr 153
Sturla Sighvatsson 52, 53
Sturla Thórdarson 57
Svava Jakobsdóttir 197
Svavar Gestsson 165
Sveinbjörn Egilsson 112, 113
Sveinbjörn Sveinbjörnsson
113
Sveinn Björnsson 142, 150,
158, 160, 161, 163
Sveinn Pálsson 88, 96
Sverrir Sigurdsson 57

Teitur Ísleifsson 42
Thangbrandur 29
Thor Vilhjálmsson 197, 198
Thorfinnur Thórdarson 27
Thorgeir of Ljósavatn 30
Thorgeir Thorgeirson 197
Thorgils Bödvarsson 55
Thorgils Gjallandi/Jón
Stefánsson 122
Thorlákur Thórhallsson
46, 47
Thormódur Torfason 84
Thorsteinn Erlingsson 122,
131
Thorsteinn Ingólfsson 20
Thorsteinn Pálsson 164, 167,
169

Thorvaldur the Far-Travelled
29
Thorvaldur Thoroddsen 129
Thórainn Nefjólfsson 35
Thórarinn B Thorláksson 153
Thórbergur Thórdarson 153
Thórdur Andrésson 59
Thórdur Sighvatsson 53,
54, 55
Torfhildur Holm 122
Tómas Gudmundsson 153
Tómas Saemundsson 103
Trampe (older) 98
Trampe (younger) 106
Tryggvi Gunnarsson 112, 136
Tryggvi Thórhallsson 148,
149

Uni Gardarsson 34

Úlfljótur 21

Valdemar of Denmark 62
Valtýr Gudmundsson 123,
124, 129
Vigdís Finnbogadóttir 162,
163

Ögmundur Pálsson 69
Össur Skarphédinsson 166